BANKING ON A PROMISE

The illusive story of money, debt and the banks that create it

FRANK BRUN

ISBN: 978-1-923601-07-9

Published by Vivid Publishing
A division of Fontaine Publishing Group
P.O. Box 948, Fremantle
Western Australia 6959
www.vividpublishing.com.au

NATIONAL LIBRARY OF AUSTRALIA

A catalogue record for this book is available from the National Library of Australia

Two chapters of this book have been submitted to Elsevier for publication in their Encyclopedia of Monetary Policy, Financial Markets and Banking. They are reproduced here with their permission. These chapters are: Chapter 2: Brun, F.M., 2025. Credit creation banking. In: Apergis, N. (Ed.), Encyclopedia of Monetary Policy, Financial Markets and Banking, vol. 1. Elsevier, Academic Press, pp. 419–425. https://dx.doi.org/10.1016/B978-0-44-313776-1.00219-1. Chapter 6: Brun, F.M., 2025. Reclaiming sovereignty through monetary reform: Three inquiries into sovereign money creation. In: Apergis, N. (Ed.), Encyclopedia of Monetary Policy, Financial Markets and Banking, vol. 1. Elsevier, Academic Press, pp. 593–606. https://dx.doi.org/10.1016/B978-0-44-313776-1.00231-2.

The real science of political economy, which has yet to be distinguished from the bastard science, as medicine from witchcraft, and astronomy from astrology, is that which teaches nations to desire and labour for the things that lead to life; and which teaches them to scorn and destroy the things that lead to destruction.

(Ruskin J. 1921, *Unto This Last*)

Table of Contents

To my grandchildren Rafael, Emily, Sofia and Michael

Preface

I started as a trainee dealer in Foreign Exchange in January 1973. As an 18-year-old keen to see the world I was extremely excited by this opportunity. I assumed since I was employed by a foreign bank, that after a while I would be exchanged for somebody in a foreign country. That may well be a little bit of tongue in cheek, but it was reflective of the extent of my knowledge of FX, and it was also the beginning of a relationship with financial markets that would see me through my entire career to my retirement in 2012 - 40 years later.

Over this time, I began my trading career being a 'spot' trader; that is buying and selling currencies whilst reacting to news and events affecting my (and the bank's) view of the currency's direction. Quick turnaround of currency positions, whilst making liquidity for the bank's clients as well as supporting the broader market, was the name of the game. I have been lucky enough to have worked for some of the world's most prestigious names in banking. Rather than banking, I should say 'risk taking'. One bank based in New York had a weekly market meeting where all the global branches would tune in by phone (this was in 1990 after all). I was in the room when a particular view was espoused on a certain currency. Within 5 minutes that bank had committed to a USD 1 billion bet against that currency! To my limited knowledge back then I felt that I had arrived in risk taking nirvana. What could go wrong? It was a win/win bet. If the bank got it right, there would be huge bonuses all around. If it got it wrong, well the balance sheet would take the hit initially, and if it got bad enough there was always the taxpayer.

Gradually my natural instincts for research led me towards wanting to cohabit with the longer-term trends to be found amongst all the noise of the intra-day apparent randomness. I migrated from initially simple point and figure reversal charts to a deep study of the Elliott Wave Theory, as the means and rationale for taking on risk for the Bank. Over the last 15 years of my career, I fine-tuned an inherent appetite to systematically analyse market trends, and how to recognise the real stuff from the biases that crept into the numbers. The idea was to remove the 'human' aspect to trading by modelling how and when to place bets, as well as managing the capital available so that overtime a sought-after return could be achieved. Researching past market action, I discovered, could be a great indicator, though not necessarily a predictor, of what to expect not only today, but also how the future may evolve. A traded price of a commodity on a reputable exchange is a recorded fact. Pure and simple. You cannot go back and change the terms of the transaction. In examining the universe of trades for a particular commodity, price, volume, volatility etc., were all considered. I learnt to recognise certain price patterns that led to certain activity that on average, and with careful risk apportioning, could lead to profitable trades over time. There were of course plenty of times when everything changed and a new paradigm was inserted into the markets that had to be analysed and coded for future reflection.

Here I am now just turned 70 and instead of trading the financial markets I am writing about them. After retirement I started studying at the University of Sydney and from 2013 to 2016 I completed a Bachelor of Political, Economic and Social Sciences, or BPESS as it is referred to. It was a combination of Political Economy, Anthropology, Government and International Relations and Writing. What a great degree that was and put together in the blender of a university degree, at such a great institution as USyd, it was an eye opener. Yes, this old dog was learning new tricks, and it provided a strong foundation for my next degree. I completed my Masters by Research in Political Economy from 2018 to 2022 - 'Credit Creation Banking: a licence to print money within the paradox of debt'. This book is the essence of that project. It is important for me to get its message out as the foundation for my next book. There is a story to all this, and it did not happen by accident.

I have found that researching the evolution of the history of the world, which of course includes the evolution of financial markets, is fraught with obfuscation and survivorship bias. It has proven to me that we do exist within a thought bubble, written by the victors of the various conflicts that have formed the global system in which we live today. As I have come to believe, political systems are born and bred from the economic systems that first sprung from the need for trade and acquisition. Through continuous myth creation and repetition generating what is referred to as the 'illusory truth effect', the winners of these conflicts (taking instruction from their money masters), tell the tale and build the myths. So again, I have had to ensure that the story that I want to tell is the real story - not the one dictated by the official narrative. It is difficult to be confronted with a refutation of the platforms and beliefs that hold us together today. But there it is. My story will be laid out to you, and I will be successful if it prompts you to question and to undertake your own research. To that end, I have purposefully left the many citations and references in the endnotes, to help the reader pursue their own version of the truth.

Acknowledgements

This book is the essence of my Masters Thesis - *Credit Creation Banking: a licence to print money within the paradox of debt* - submitted in early 2022 to the University of Sydney. I am grateful to that wonderful institution, and especially my supervisor throughout that project, Mike Beggs. Thank you for teaching an old dog new tricks and any remaining faults are mine to own

I wish to thank my daughters Alex and Nicole for their support and many inspirational and materially helpful discussions.

When I look back over my long career there are many names and faces that come to mind as having influenced my thinking about markets and life in general. In particular, and early on when I was still fumbling along, was a guy called Peter Arnott ('biscuits'). Peter taught me much about the markets, the EWT and how to read between the lines of life. Stuff that I carry still today, nearly fifty years later. He sadly passed many years ago, but Peter you are still in my thoughts and my path would have been vastly different had we not met.

Finally, to my wife Marina – thanks for always being there for me.

Abstract

The essence of the capitalist engine is the ability by banks to be able to create credit money on nothing but a promise to repay. Money, as the universal medium of exchange, is the lifeblood of modern society. As such it is too important a common good to be left to private, commercial and profit seeking enterprises called 'Banks' to issue and control through their balance sheets. Similarly to law-and-order, education, defence or health the issue and control of a stable and reliable medium of exchange is a Sovereign responsibility. It is a prerequisite for the effective functioning and management of society in a fair and equitable manner.

This book investigates whether the two major financial crises of the last 100 years are symptomatic of the fact that money is just too important to be left to banks to create simply through the issuance of debt. The Great Depression, beginning after the stock market crash of 1929, and then the Great Financial Crisis (GFC) of 2007/09, were the stimulants for two major debates on monetary reform. This study addresses these debates firstly through the lens of three great economic thinkers of the 1930s, Henry Simons, Frank Knight and Irving Fisher, and their assertions on the newly elected Roosevelt Government to mandate a 100% Full Reserve Banking (100%FRB) system.

Then it will pursue the arguments mounted post GFC for a Sovereign Money System (SMS) by various nations. Under the SMS, government as the sovereign entity is to reclaim the responsibility for the issuance of the medium of exchange. This book seeks common threads between these two enquiries into monetary reform. It seeks confirmation or otherwise of the assertion that economic inequality and volatility, leading to economic crisis, arises as a result of the endogenous contradiction of the capitalist system. That is, the creation of money through debt issuance.

Chapter 1
Introduction

1.1 Introduction

On 10th June 2018 Switzerland held a people's initiative in the form of a binding referendum on whether to instigate a Sovereign Money system. Its aim was to segregate the monetary and credit functions of the banking system by removing the power from commercial banks to create the medium of exchange through debt issuance, and place that power solely within the Swiss government via the Swiss National Bank (Dawnay, 2017). Although it received very little publicity externally, it was the most serious attempt towards monetary and banking reform since a group of Chicago school economists led by Frank Knight and Henry Simons, as well as Irving fisher from Yale put forward their plans for change to the nascent Roosevelt administration. In the early 1930s, in what has collectively come to be known as the Chicago Plan, these academics amongst many others also proposed the separation of banks' money creating from money lending powers. The Chicago Plan wanted a 100% reserve requirement to be imposed on the banking system by requiring that bank deposits be totally backed by some sort of risk-free government-issued money (Phillips, 1995). These inquiries were motivated by a belief that an economic system with a media of exchange, appearing in the form of self-generated bank liabilities, is inherently unstable (Knight, 1927; Fisher, 1936; Simons 1948; Turner, 2010; Werner, 2014; Huber, 2017 (a)). The aim of this book is to critically review and compare the arguments put forward by these two inquiries. This thesis concludes that the consequences of a private banking industry having the power to influence the money supply, which is essentially a public good, are too socially important to render the process completely in the hands of commercial banks.

From the mid nineteenth century when the English Banking Act of 1844 was enacted, the debates between the currency and the banking schools focused on how the media of exchange should be created. Should it be a creation of the state, governed by a strict set of rules, as the currency school would argue? Or should it be left to private enterprise and allowed the flexibility to respond to the needs of entrepreneurs, as the banking school argued (Goodhart and Jensen, 2015)? This question is at the core of the Chicago Plan and Sovereign money inquiries into monetary reform. Frederick Soddy, the 1921 Nobel Laureate in Chemistry had already written in his 1926 book *Wealth, Virtual Wealth and Debt* that "[t]he only way banking today can be made safe both for the banker and the nation is for the nation to be the banker" (Soddy 1933:13). Soddy is credited with reviving the discussion around 100% reserve banking, although it was an argument already acknowledged by many academics of the 1930s. Prior to Soddy there had been previous attempts at full reserves banking, for example Laina (2015) points to the U.K. Bank Charter Act 1844 mentioned above, and the National Acts of 1863 and 1864 in the U.S. These acts were attempts by the proponents of the Currency school to place rules around money creation. These acts failed to understand and foresee the ability of banks to circumvent these rules by generating alternate means of settling transactions, for example in the form of chequing deposits. As Frank Vanderlip states in section 2.3 below, the median of exchange was already in 1908, 95% bank liabilities.

Money, as I will demonstrate, enters the economy through debt issuance by banks. It therefore follows that since too much debt precedes economic crises, that they eventuate as a consequence of too much money creation (Ravn 2021). Karl Marx heralded Irving fisher's *Debt Deflation Theory* (1933) when he wrote about this in Capital Volume III (Marx 1909: 372):

> In a system of production, in which the entire connection of the process of reproduction rests upon credit, a crisis must obviously occur through a tremendous rush for means of payment, when credit suddenly ceases and nothing but cash payment goes.

The Federal Reserve System (FED) created in December 1913 seems to specifically address Marx's point above in that the rush for cash by depositors, would allow the banks to call on the FED to replenish their depleted and highly geared reserves as required. It may well be that an expanding economy does benefit from an expanding money supply, however the construct of society has evolved to one where this expanding money supply is fed by credit. As things currently stand this credit is a liability not of the core asset holder in the economy, the government, but of intervening private enterprises, the commercial banks and the shadow banks. This mercurial development of a dual money system (Huber, 2017 (b)) is the keystone to ongoing financial instability and crisis because as Marx alludes to above, from time to time we are done with the secondary money issued by banks as their self-created liabilities and wish to secure our wealth to the commons through primary money. I see this act as a primeval search for security that will continue to wash over society unless structural reform is enacted over current monetary practices.

1.2 Aim and Structure of this book

In chapter 2 we follow the banking school view as we deal with the rise and establishment of credit creation banking in the United States. We move quickly through banking arrangement in the 19th century to the passing of the Federal Reserve Act in December 1913. We touch on a conference convened at Columbia University by Professor Edwin Seligman in 1908 (Columbia, 1908). This group of leading bankers espoused their solution to the problems facing the growing U.S. economy from the existing system of decentralised reserves, as being the establishment of a central reserves entity. Before the creation of the Federal Reserve System gold, silver and currency represented the reserves of the banking system. Banks could borrow from each other, but this represented the circulation of existing reserves, not the creation of new ones (FED BG 1939). This acted to slow the increase of funding required by the growing economy since banks could not substantially increase lending, due to a lack of new reserves. Of interest is the clarity of the submission by a leading banker of the times, Frank Vanderlip, postulating that the financing of the expansionary industrial economy was not through a process where deposits generated loans but rather one where loans created deposits.

Chapter 3 begins with the stock market highs of 1929 and the subsequent collapse, which eventually led to the Great Depression in the 1930s. I detail some empirical observations around the extent of the economic collapse and the proposals for change that emanated from that event. This chapter puts forward the currency school arguments for monetary reform through the lens of the thinking of three highly respected laissez faire economists, Frank Knight, Henry Simons and Irving Fisher, and the proposals for monetary reform they put to the Roosevelt administration. I pursue the contradiction that laissez faire, neoclassical scholars believed that banks needed to be hamstrung in their capacity to increase and decrease the money supply. The contradiction lies in the fact that these writers on monetary reform in the 1930s believed, that for capitalism to survive as it is intended, it must be allowed to thrive within the constraints and rules placed upon it by the publicly elected authorities. Frank Knight especially draws on Frederick Soddy's writings on this issue. The common theme that connects the Chicago Plan writings of the 1930s to the Sovereign Money debates of the 2010s is that too much debt has implications for the behaviour of individuals and the economy at large . We conclude this chapter by examining the policy outcomes that emanated from the Roosevelt administration's New Deal banking reforms.

Chapter 4 looks at the theory underpinning bank balance sheets. Banking has evolved radically over the hundred years or so covered by this thesis. I needed to include a theoretical chapter on the mechanisms of banking to provide an insight and understanding of the changing money flows. For example, I describe how an initial deposit of $10,000 can be transformed into $100,000 of bank liabilities and purchasing power through fractional reserve banking. In placing this theoretical chapter midway through the story, the transition in banking practices is made clearer. The development of banking since the establishment of the Federal Reserve in 1913 goes hand in hand with theories on the determination of the money supply provided through the writings of Chick (1992) and Goodhart (2017). I look at the hierarchy of the creation of the money supply and how the multiplier system worked in the past. Through Werner (2014) we begin to understand how a bank can generate a deposit and its subsequent spending power through bookkeeping. A bank can also do the reverse. We also, through the work of LSE economist Roger Alford (Alford 2010) get a simplified understanding of the critical bank ratios, the solvency and liquidity ratios. Using data from the Board of Governors of the Federal Reserve we can apply the Alford technique (henceforth the "Alford Cross") and visualise the fragilities of the U.S. Banking system in the 1930s. We also use the Alford Cross technique to apply the Chicago Plan proposals of dismantling the banking powers to lend the money that they create. We arrive at the conclusion that bank gearing of equity and liquidity lies at the heart of financial crises.

In chapter 5 'Can it Happen Again' we move from the 1930s financial crash and Great Depression to the Great Financial Crisis of the 2000's. Using the Board of Governors of the Federal Reserve System data, updated from 1914 to present time, we analyse the development of banking liquidity and solvency ratios over two distinct periods. These are defined as the Golden Era of Capitalism from the post New Deal period to the late 1970s commencement of the neoliberal relaxation of banking regulations. The next period, the Neoliberal Era is defined by the extraordinary growth in debt to GDP. We examine the reasons and repercussions of this growth in debt. Along the way we pause to examine the rescue of the then seventh largest bank, Continental Illinois National Bank in 1984. The Congressional report into this rescue provides a good insight into the development of the banking and regulatory relationships, as the strictures of the New Deal banking acts are gradually watered down. It was the first occurrence of the 'too big to fail' terminology as applied to bank rescues. We then examine the Great Financial Crisis and the Financial Crisis Inquiry Commission report into that failure. Minsky (1957) and Mehrling (2011), as well as Kohn (2010) add insights into the historical comparisons of the two crises. The origins, evolution and importance of the alternate 'shadow banking' industry are examined. We conclude this chapter with the observation that both financial crises were spurred by too much debt and not enough of liquidity.

In chapter 6 we compare the two proposals for monetary reform, the Chicago Plan of the 1930s and the Sovereign Money inquiries of the 2010s. We find significant differences between the two proposals although their eventual purpose is the same. We rely on Huber (2015, 2017 (a), (b), (c)) and Dyson (et al. 2016) for explanations on Sovereign Money Creation (SMC). For purposes of the latter inquiries, we look at reports from the United States, Iceland and Switzerland. We draw on the work of Nobel laureate and Henry Simons' student James Buchanan, for an understanding of 'constitutional money' as support for SMC. The corner stone of the SMC argument is that the current dual money system needs to revert to a single money sovereign system. The insertion of the banking industry between the individual and the repository of his wealth needs to be redressed. Finally, we consider the work being currently done by central banks around the globe investigating the possibility of Central Bank Digital Currencies. Is this a way forward for SMC?

Chapter 2
Credit Creation Banking

2.1 Introduction

To understand capitalism we need to understand that credit, leading to deposits, which are exchangeable for and as money,[2] emanates through banks[3], and it is measured through accounting (Bezemer 2016).[4] Banking as a system producing credit, the lifeblood of capitalism, is in fact banking on a promise. It is a promise by the bank to pay the borrower present value flows as deposits on demand. In return, it is a promise by the borrower to pay the bank from future income flows. It is a system that needs to be understood in any examination of monetary arrangements in our exchange society. Chapter 2 Credit Creation Banking will briefly deal with the early evolvement of monetary arrangements in the United States up to the formation of the Federal Reserve System in December 1913. America was the last major developed nation to establish a central bank and finally after two previous attempts[6] the banking fraternity won out. Prior to the establishment of central banking in America its growing economy was hamstrung for credit. There were no lender of last resort facilities and banks were reticent to provide the credit required for the expanding economy. The financial crisis of 1907[7] demonstrated the dangers that banks faced if they met the demands for debt of a growing nation. The Columbia University conferences in 1907/08 to discuss the currency problem facing the country were motivated by the crisis of the time. Subsequently through strong lobbying to the newly elected Wilson administration, the Federal Reserve Act was passed in December 1913.

2.2: Towards Credit Creation Banking

Towards the turn of the twentieth century American monetary arrangements could well be described as organised chaos. In a nation that had been born in the country but had moved to the cities (Johnson 2010) popular distrust of eastern seaboard banks and money men had ensured not only the absence of any European style central bank, but also a multifarious system of state and national banks, as well as country, reserve and central reserve arrangements (Singleton 2010) that created a diverse and, according to the bankers of the time, a weakened system incapable of funding the needs of the nascent power. The absence of a central bank, since the expiration of the Charter of the Second Bank of the United States in 1836, meant that 'America's financial picture was increasingly characterized by inelastic currency and immobile reserves' (Johnson 2010: 14). In what was an early precursor to 100% reserves banking, the National Banking act of 1863 had instituted the requirement for National banks to carry United States government securities in full support of banknotes issued (Johnson 2010: 12).[8] This served to fund the North's efforts during the American civil war but it also led to a currency in circulation that was primarily influenced by the value of the bonds underpinning it, rather than the ebb and flow of commercial business demands (Singleton 2010).

At the end of the 19th and beginning of the 20th centuries the inability of the currency to fluctuate according to the natural expansionary demands of a burgeoning economy was becoming critical (Singleton 2010: 52). America was at the threshold of an explosive expansionary phase and yet the inflexible currency and scattered reserves across 50 cities acted as a break on the credit demands that were required to fund it. As Johnson puts it:

> [i]t had become clear that the national banking system did not provide the regulating mechanism for money and banking that the two Banks of the United States had provided early in the nation's history. And as the American economy became larger, more urban, and more complex, the inelastic currency and the immobile reserves contributed to the cyclical pattern of booms and busts. These wide gyrations were becoming more and more intolerable. (Johnson 2010: 15)

The severe financial panic of 1907 caused several banks to fail. It did not lead to a broader economic collapse, but it did lead to the question of the nation's banking arrangements once again coming to the forefront of national debate. The two previous combatants lined themselves up yet again for the perennial battle. That is, the populist progressives representing farmers and small businesses, and the conservatives representing the powerful business and banking groups of the eastern cities.

The financial crisis of 1907 had been preceded by crises in 1893, 1890, 1879 and 1873. According to Groseclose (1976: 205) 'At each crisis, the principal remedy advocated was a further expansion of the money system, a stronger dose of the tonic of cheap money and cheap credit.' The country was hungry for purchasing power and the way to achieve it, in a system where the issuance of currency was hamstrung by the need to own government bonds in equal measures, was through bank credit. As already mentioned, by the turn of the 20th century, the National Banking Act was acting as a handbrake on a fast car, and something had to change. The economic debate up until the early 1900s had been how much power to give the banks to create the medium of exchange and thus generate purchasing power. It was the historic debate between the currency school and the banking school.[9] The currency school believed the banking roles of money creation and money intermediation should be separate and distinct. They wanted the money supply to be a state issued monopoly and its growth to be managed through a rules-based system. The banking school on the other hand believed that only private institutions were able to gauge the needs of commerce to expand and contract.[10] They believed the growth or contraction in the money supply had to be flexible according to the ebb and flow of industry (Goodhart & Jensen 2015). In further support of this we turn to the thinking of leading bankers and financiers, as they gave a series of presentations at Columbia University over the autumn of 1907 and the spring of 1908 (Moore 1909).

2.3: The Columbia University Lectures (1908)

Organised by Columbia University professor Edwin Seligman, these lectures were compiled into a booklet and were titled *The Currency Problem and the Present Financial Situation* (Columbia 1908). The conference was motivated by a desire amongst like-minded financiers and academics to investigate the causes of the 1907 crisis; the roots of which were believed to be in the inflexibility of the currency, and the solution in common was seen to be the establishment of a reservoir of reserves via a central bank (Moore 1909). Regarding economic crises, Seligman wrote in the introduction to the Columbia (1908) pamphlet that crises were modern phenomena. In America the first economic crisis was in 1817, in England before that, in 1763. Seligman attributed economic crises to modern economic life, which he said, 'has as its basal characteristic industrial capitalism, with the factory system and the newer methods of production for a wide market' (Columbia 1908: x). Investigating the sources for these modern economic crises, Seligman refuted the theories of overproduction or underconsumption.

Instead, he led his discussion towards the argument that modern production is enacted en masse towards a wide and varied market. Consequently, the 'problem of crises or industrial depressions is one of overcapitalisation' (Columbia 1908: xiii) as producers invested in the expectation of making a profit, rather than with a predetermined order in place.[11]

As Seligman wrote, 'In times of buoyancy we are continually capitalizing anticipated earnings and future hopes, and we do this through the utilization of credit on a large scale' (Columbia 1908: xiv). So, for Seligman industrial capitalism was fuelled by the capitalisation of future income streams using bank credit. The naturally optimistic nature of the entrepreneur, or perhaps through over stretched greed, however, would lead to the overcapitalisation of future incomes. This in turn leads to reassessment and readjustment of investments in production. Thus, according to Seligman, it is always some extraneous event that leads to the overcapitalised house of cards to come tumbling down. It is not the endogenous over creation of money through over lending by banks. Extending this line of thought, an economic crisis would eventuate as a natural retraction of a previously overenthusiastic expansion of capitalisation.[12] The two theories proposed by the banking school and the currency school adherents appear to be pivotal around a central point of blame. The bankers blame the capitalist entrepreneur for overextending himself, seeing their own role as simply greasing the wheels of industry.[13] That is the banking school argument. The currency school argument, as we will soon see being posed by Knight, Simons and Fisher, saw the problem as being the bank overextending itself through its aggressive balance sheet expansion and then its subsequent contraction.

The speech from Frank A. Vanderlip was an important contribution to the same conference.[14] Vanderlip was Assistant Secretary, US Treasury, 1897–1901 and President, National City Bank, 1909–1919[15]. His lecture contribution to the Columbia (1908) volume was simply titled *The Modern Bank*. He refers to the all too frequent occurrence of financial crises in America as:

> In no other great nation of the world are such financial catastrophes regularly enacted. Nowhere else may be found an important financial system subject to such violent turbulence as is the money market of the United States. (Columbia 1908: 3)

For Vanderlip American finance was severely hamstrung and the country could learn much from the evolution of financial systems in England and Europe. Coming from one of the important and central figures in finance at the turn of the 20th century, Vanderlip's description of the business of banking is quite illuminating. He agreed with Seligman and all the other financiers that within their formalist, neoclassical economy, the free market led self-interested maximisers to seek personal gain.[16] Under this system money was neutral. It was simply a means of payment.

It is worth quoting Vanderlip in detail as he describes how finance and banking operated in America at the turn of the 20th century:

> The money transactions of a bank are, under ordinary conditions, comparatively insignificant: almost its entire business consists of receiving from its customers their evidences of indebtedness, which have a narrow currency, and giving to those customers in exchange the bank's evidences of indebtedness, which have a wide currency. These evidences of a bank's indebtedness are then transferred from one individual to another and from one bank to another, and in that way the credits created serve the purpose of the medium of exchange by which perhaps ninety-five per cent of the exchange transactions of commerce take place (Columbia 1908: 5).[17]

The evidence of indebtedness referred to can be taken as the customer's liability or potential liability. On this alone the bank would generate the purchasing power to be passed on to the customer through a loan. Thus, the customer could go ahead and fulfill their plans.[18] Vanderlip explains further that savings are not first deposited in the bank, and the bank then lends these savings out. As he says, 'The operation is the reverse. The bank first makes a loan to the borrower and in so doing creates a deposit.' (Columbia 1908: 5). It is interesting to consider that although since the late 19th century the debate around money has been pushed into the heterodox sphere,[19] Vanderlip was stating in 1908 that loans lead to deposits and that therefore investments accordingly led to savings, not the other way around.[20] We will soon see that such power over the money supply leads to financial instability affecting the entire country, making money far from 'neutral'. As quoted above, it is important to take away from this that even more than one hundred years ago, 95% of the medium of exchange, or what was accepted as money, was very conveniently carried out by cheques drawn on deposits generated by the banks (Columbia 1908). As Vanderlip suggests above, the issuing of banknotes was insignificant compared to the issuing of chequing accounts. This was already credit creation banking. It had become clear that the bank's role was not to lend money; the bank's role was to interpose its debt for that of the client's.

2.4: The Creation of the FED (1913) - The Capstone on an International Credit Money System

Some years later, in a speech delivered to the Investment Bankers Association of America on October 30, 1913 (Vanderlip 1913), Vanderlip laid out what were the true plans of the country's financiers and bankers. By this stage the debate of the Federal Reserve Act Bill was almost complete and Vanderlip had been testifying before congress for three days. Finally, he was asked to prepare a plan for a Central Bank. In his speech Vanderlip outlined that the crucial requirement for the advancement of American finance, and thus American industry, was

> the creation of a central reserve reservoir. I think there is pretty universal agreement that that is the great fundamental thing which is necessary in our banking system. (Vanderlip 1913: 2).[21]

The other crucial factor being the requirement for the currency to be flexible. It needed to expand and contract according to the demands of commerce. The defining legislation, which was to be passed on December 23, 1913, was known as the Federal Reserve Act or the Glass-Owen Bill. This act created the third central bank in the United States and unlike the first two it very much remains in place over 100 years later.

The passage of the Federal Reserve Act however was not without controversy. The panics of 1873, 1893 and 1907 had instilled in the American public a sense that the financial and industrial tycoons on the east coast were not to be trusted with the nation's finances (Alcorn 2014). This had led to what was known as the Progressive struggle in American politics. One of the most prominent detractors from the Bill was the Republican Representative from Minnesota, Charles A. Lindbergh. In his book *Banking and Currency and the Money Trust* (1913) Lindbergh claimed that the 1907 financial panic was staged by the banks to facilitate the Federal Reserve legislation. He wrote (Lindbergh 1913: 33):

> [t]here is a man-made god that controls the social and industrial system that governs us. We know him as the "Money Trust"... At the present time he has an almost illimitable influence upon our daily actions and is seeking to increase it by framing new currency and banking laws to suit his purposes.

The eventual passing of the Federal Reserve Act in 1913 was the laying of the capstone, finally, on the evolution of a system of finance from the early beginnings of the formation of the Bank of England in 1694,[22] to the system that we have today. It was a system that was portrayed by the banking school adherents as being most capable of meeting the requirements for purchasing power of a growing industrial capitalism. The ultimate means for doing this was through their ability to create a medium of exchange function through issuing bank liabilities. This power was further enhanced through the establishment of a central bank in the United States. Furthermore, the credit creation of the medium of exchange had to be fully removed from any sovereign interference. Thus, in the Federal Reserve Act of December 1913 (the Act), Congress granted the Federal Reserve Bank (the FED) the power to create unlimited money. Phillips (2014: 236) quotes Section 16 of the original Act:

> Federal Reserve notes, to be issued at the discretion of the Federal Reserve Board for the purpose of making advances to Federal reserve banks through the Federal reserve agents as hereinafter set forth and for no other purpose, are hereby authorized. The said notes shall be obligations of the United States and shall be receivable by all national and member banks and Federal Reserve banks and for all taxes, customs, and other public dues.

Griffin (1998) adds a further twist to this granting of legal tender status to Federal Reserve Notes by Congress. This is in the form of a quote from the 'father' of the Federal Reserve Act, Paul Warburg. Griffin quotes Warburg:

> While technically and legally the Federal Reserve note is an obligation of the United States Government, in reality it is an obligation, the sole actual responsibility for which rests

> on the reserve banks.... The government could only be called upon to take them up after the reserve banks had failed (Griffin 1998: 466).

Griffin writes that Warburg's assertion was that '*Federal Reserve notes constitute privately issued money with the taxpayers standing by to cover the potential losses of those banks which issue it.*' (Griffin 1998: 467, italics in original). This line of argument proposed by Griffin deserves to be pursued further but it cannot be done here. However, if this was Warburg's true sentiment then he was possessed with amazing foresight since that has been the fact ever since the passing of the Federal Reserve Act in 1913.

2.5 Conclusion

Chapter 2 has sought to lay the scene for the important part that banking plays in the social and economic organisation of society. The primary means by which it does so is simply because in what is essentially a market society, the media of exchange comes from the issuance of debt by the banking industry. That is, the media of exchange is created through the process of credit creation banking. This leads to the importance of accounting in today's interaction between finance and reproduction. The existence of this came about through the gradual encroaching of the banking industry into the traditional sovereign sphere of the issuance of the means of exchange. As we have seen the nascent and expanding American economy needed the flexibility that a credit money system would provide. The Columbia University conference speeches were part of the efforts of the banking school to gain and lock-in the rights to this money production. In this section we have focused on Vanderlip's paper, but Warburg and the other conferees' contributions were just as important, and all posed the same goal. That goal was that the creation of the money supply should be left in the hands of the banks. Further a central bank was required to act as a backstop to smooth out the periods of volatility that came along from time to time, as entrepreneurs erased their prior over-enthusiastic activity, causing bank lending to firstly overextend, but then to contract.

It has been further proposed here that the creation of the Federal Reserve System was the capstone in a global credit system that had already been in place in Europe but needed to be finally cemented into place in North America, for it to become a true system of global finance. The rest of this essay will consider the impact if any, that this power to coin money by private, profit seeking institutions, has had on the evolvement of economic society through the twentieth century to today. As we will see, this evolution of banking on a promise has been punctuated by financial crises of varying degrees; the two outstanding ones being the Great Depression of the 1930s, and the Global Financial Crisis of 2007/2009. What part did banks play in these two major financial crises? Albert Hart believed, as he wrote in Hart & Mehrling 1995: 8:

> This view of banking as a balancing act which occasionally breaks down in cumulative expansion or contraction leads naturally to a view of business fluctuations as driven by the instability of credit.

Banks, according to Hart were predominant in their responsibility for economic volatility.

The endogenous creation of money by the banking system is the backbone of capitalism.[23] It is the truth behind capitalism, and capitalism would not have been able to become the dominant economic paradigm without it. As Ingham quotes Schumpeter in 'Capitalism' (2008: 71) "'the development of the law and practice of negotiable paper and of "created" deposits is the best indication we have for the rise of capitalism'". What is really happening here, and it was alluded to by Vanderlip above, is that banks are standing in between their client the borrower, and their client's creditor. Banks are becoming the repositories of almost all (95% according to Vanderlip) end arrangements that involve exchange. They are doing this because their liability, the deposit granted to the client, is accepted in payment by other clients and their clients and so on. Money has been replaced by the bank's liability. The medium of exchange is no longer a value icon such as a commodity; it is a bank reputation and name, or in other words a bank debt. This reputation was sorely tested, if not ruined, during the boom-and-bust periods of the late 1920s and early 1930s thus setting the scene for the revival of the currency school side of this perennial monetary debate. We will now see this through the lens of three great economic thinkers of the 1930s, as we study the depressed years of the 1930s and what proposals were sought to curb the banks' power to create money through debt.

Chapter 3

First Debate on Monetary Reform: The Chicago Plan of Banking Reform and the Paradox of Debt

3.1 Introduction

From its peak in early September 1929 of 381.17, to the trough in mid-July 1932 of 42.68 the primary stock market indicator in the United States, the Dow Jones Index, lost 89% in value. This was symptomatic of a wider financial calamity that was to befall the U.S.A., and the world, over the subsequent decade. In the second section of this chapter, *Proposals for Change*, we assess the extent of the financial crisis of the 1930s and then consider the proposals for change put forward in 1933 by various academics from the University of Chicago,[24] subsequently named the Chicago Plan for Banking Reform.[25] The Chicago Plan was a proposal for the dramatic transformation of finance and banking in the United States in the 1930s, promoted amongst others by two highly respected neoclassical, laissez faire Chicago economists, Frank Knight and Henry Simons.[26] Amongst other measures, it was a plan to separate the deposit creating from the lending functions within commercial banks (Knight et al. 1933). A similar argument was later developed by arguably the leading American economist of the time, Irving

Fisher from Yale, with his '100% Money' proposal (Fisher 1936). The philosophical groundings supporting the calls for policy change in banking arrangements, put forward by these two proposals are investigated in the third section of this chapter through the lens of the writings of these three prominent economists.

The Chicago Plan and 100% Money arguments fall within the ambit of the Currency School belief that the creation of money and the intermediation of money are in fact two very separate roles that could easily be carried out by two separate institutions (Knight et al. 1933, Fisher 1936, Phillips 1995, Goodhart & Jensen 2015). The British Banking Act of 1844[27] was an early attempt to reform banking to comply with the separation of these two functions. Paradoxically however, instead of curtailing the expansion of money by banks the Act created the impetus for its vast expansion. Commercial banking would not be curtailed by the limitations on note issue imposed by the Act;[28] instead it developed alternate measures to add liquidity to an expanding European economy through the creation of chequing deposits - otherwise known as near money (Goodhart & Jensen 2015, Fontana & Sawyer 2016). As chapter 2 has shown the Banking school adherents wanted monetary flexibility. Banking school supporters believed that 'the financial system is evolutionary, not static, and a rule adopted in one set of circumstances may soon become out-dated and inappropriate' (Goodhart & Jensen 2015: 21). This chapter deals mainly with the currency school view, that is a money system with the objective of the 'abolition of private credit as an element in the circulating media' and with the 'concentration of complete and direct control over the quantity of media in the hands of the central monetary authority' (Simons quoted in Allen 1993: 706).

Knight, Simons and Fisher, all liberal, laissez faire neoclassical thinkers, believed as Hart wrote about Hawtry's teachings, 'that any disturbance to the economy tends to be magnified by the credit system' (Hart & Mehrling (1995: 3). They further believed that '[f] or understanding financial instability, it is important to start from the fact that bank lending creates money' (Hart & Mehrling (1995: 6). Therefore, as we will see, radical change was required to the banking system to avoid the re-occurrence of the economic crisis in which these economists found themselves enmeshed. In the fourth section of this chapter we will look at some of the policy outcomes that emanated as a result of their efforts. Although as will be seen, Fisher and his 100% Money was prepared to leave banks largely untroubled, and Knight and Simons through the Chicago Plan wanted a complete reorganisation and transformation of banking, they all believed in a rules-based system for the addition of new money into the economy, albeit through different paths. Further, although the 100% Reserve Banking (henceforth 100%RB) arguments proposed by the Chicago Plan were identical to Fisher's 100% money plan in that the state was to have sole responsibility for the creation or destruction of the money supply, as we will see the two plans differed fundamentally in some important respects (Demeulemeester 2018). The fifth section concludes.

3.2 The Chicago Plan and 100% Money - Proposals for Change

3.2.1 The economic crisis of the 1930s

Taking 1914 as the start year (the creation of the Federal Reserve Bank System), Table 3.2.1 and Figure 3.2.1[29] show the growth in certain financial indicators over the fifteen years from 1914 to the peak of the stock market in 1929, and the subsequent crash over the ensuing four years to the trough of 1933.[30] Figure 3.2.2[31] shows this volatility as a drawdown chart. The charts reflect what we will soon see in the writings on Simons, Knight and Fisher. That is, the banking practice of increasing the money supply by generating deposits through loans during the up cycles; and then decreasing the money supply during downturns as loans are repaid and bank lending is reduced. This is promoted in this essay as an important causal factor in the market volatility that ensued post 1929. For example, as Table 3.2.1 shows the fall in total bank risk assets of 29.8% from 1929 to 1933 was matched by a fall in total bank deposits over the same period of 28.5%. Correspondingly there was a fall in bank capital of 26.1% as well as a fall in liquidity of 29.2%. The impact from the decline in these bank ratios[32] flowed onto money supply and risky markets such as the Dow Jones Index.[33] There was a subsequent deflationary (see Fisher below) crash, as shown in Table 3.2.1 that saw the CPI fall by 24.3% and nominal GDP fall by 45.3%. It is important to bear in mind not just the sheer size of the financial collapse but the short period that it took to complete - that is four years from 1929 to 1933.

Table 3.2.1 Growth/Decline in certain financial measures Dec 1914 to Dec 1933

	Total Earning Assets (Banks - Millions $)	Total Capital (Banks - Millions $)	Solvency Ratio	Total Deposits (Banks - Millions $)	Total Liquid Assets* (Banks - Millions $)	Liquidity Ratio	Money Supply** (Deposits + Liquid Assets) $Millions	U.S. Consumer Price Index Average 1982-1984 = 100	Dow Jones Industrial Average	Nominal GDP (Millions $)	Value of $1 in 1914 to 1933 - CPI based	Velocity (GDP/Money supply)
Dec-1914	8,498	2,093	24.63%	8,305	2,500	30.10%	10,805	9.7	55	36,831	1.00	3.41
Dec-1929	35,934	6,710	18.67%	37,980	9,136	24.05%	47,116	17.1	248	104,600	0.49	2.22
Dec-1933	25,219	4,962	19.68%	27,167	6,471	23.82%	33,638	13.0	100	57,200	0.63	1.70

	Growth/ (-) Decline Total Earning Assets (Banks)	Growth/ (-) Decline Total Capital (Banks)	Growth/ (-) Decline Solvency Ratio	Growth/ (-) Decline Total Deposits (Banks)	Growth/ (-) Decline Total Liquic Assets (Banks)	Growth/ (-) Decline Liquidity Ratio	Money Supply** (Deposits + Liquid Assets) $Millions	Growth/ (-) Decline U.S. Consumer Price Index Average 1982-1984 = 100	Growth/ (-) Decline Dow Jones Industrial Average	Growth/ (-) Decline Nominal GDP	Growth/ (-) Decline Value of $1 in 1914 to 1933 - CPI based	Velocity (GDP/Money supply)
Dec 1914 Dec 1929	322.85%	220.59%	-24.18%	357.31%	265.44%	-20.09%	336.06%	76.78%	355.26%	184.00%	-51.18%	-34.87%
Dec 1929 Dec 1933	-29.82%	-26.05%	5.37%	-28.47%	-29.17%	-0.98%	-28.61%	-24.34%	-59.80%	-45.32%	29.34%	-23.40%

* https://www.federalreserve.gov/releases/H8/20200821/h8.pdf: Liquid Assets = Cash assets:"Includes vault cash, cash items in process of collection, balances due from depository institutions, and balances due from Federal Reserve Banks."

** Money Supply: 'Banking and Monetary Statistics 1914-1941 Part I'. p. 680. "The supply of money, in the sense of a means of payment, is generally defined to include currency and demand deposits of banks."

Source: FED BG Banking and Monetary Statistics 1914-1941 for banks and money supply; Measuring Worth: https://www.measuringworth.com for everything else.

Figure 3.2.1 Relative growth in certain financial measures 1914-1933

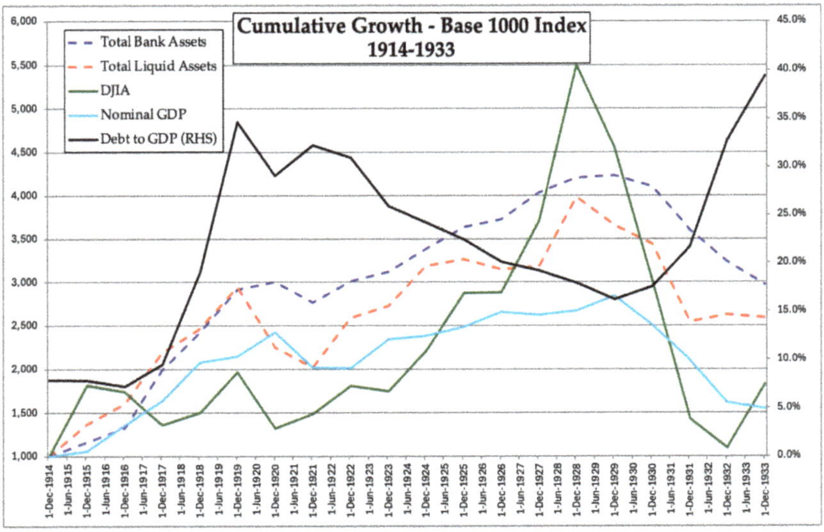

Source: FED BG Banking and Monetary Statistics 1914-1941 for banks and money supply; Measuring Worth: https://www.measuringworth.com for everything else.

Figure 3.2.2 Relative decline in certain financial measures 1914-1933

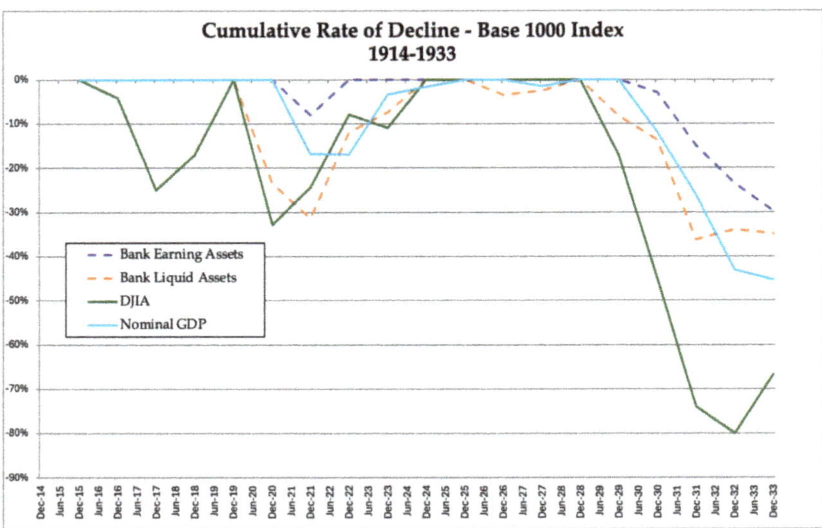

Source: FED BG Banking and Monetary Statistics 1914-1941 for banks and money supply; Measuring Worth: https://www.measuringworth.com for everything else.

As shown above, the gyrations of economic and financial indicators over the years from 1914[34] to 1933, especially when considering the number of bank suspensions and failures over the period (Table 3.2.2), were dramatic. The sharp upswings shown in Figure 3.2.1 and the subsequent violent downswings shown in the drawdown chart of Figure 3.2.2 reflect the extreme economic volatility proposed by Fisher's (1933) debt-deflation theory, as over exuberance takes the market up to a point where disequilibrium is established, leading to a retraction where misery and panic feed on themselves to some undetermined low.[35] Both of these issues are elaborated upon further in section 3.3.3 below. As a consequence of this instability, and as institutionalists,[36] the Chicago proponents of change to the banking system saw about them an economy that was failing society. Therefore, the pragmatic solution would be to design a new one. As A. G. Hart (one of the original signatories to the March 1933 document - see below) wrote in 1938:

> [t]he economy, so we thought, is a social institution created by us, and if the old economy no longer works, we must simply invent a new one that works better. (Hart AG, Mehrling P 1995: viii)

Previous attempts however at regulating the free creation of money through deposits, such as the British Bank Act 1844, and the American National Bank Acts of 1863 and 1864 had omitted the crucial fact that bank issued on demand deposits were quickly becoming the dominant money in the economy (Laina 2015: 4, Kindleberger & Aliber 2005: 67).

Table 3.2.2 Bank failures 1921:1933.

1921 - 1933: Commercial Bank Suspensions					
Year	Number of Suspensions	Deposits ($)	Losses Borne by Depositors ($)	Losses to Depositors as % of Deposits in All Suspended Banks	Losses to Depositors as % of Deposits in All Comm. Banks
1921	506	172,806	59,967	34.70	0.21
1922	366	91,182	38,223	41.92	0.13
1923	646	149,601	62,142	41.54	0.19
1924	775	210,150	79,381	37.77	0.23
1925	617	166,937	60,799	36.42	0.16
1926	975	260,153	83,066	31.93	0.21
1927	669	199,332	60,681	30.44	0.15
1928	498	142,386	43,813	30.77	0.10
1929	659	230,643	76,659	33.24	0.18
1930	1,350	837,096	237,359	28.36	0.57
1931	2,293	1,690,232	390,476	23.10	1.01
1932	1,453	706,187	168,302	23.83	0.57
1933	4,000*	3,596,708	540,396	15.02	2.15
Total	14,807*	$8,453,413	$1,901,264	22.49	5.86

*Estimate.

3.2.2 Proposals for Change

The primary objective of a memorandum, initially passed in March 1933 to Henry A. Wallace then Secretary of Agriculture to President Roosevelt, by eight leading economists from the University of Chicago was to propose permanent reforms 'effecting a complete separation, between different classes of corporations, of the Deposit and Lending functions of existing commercial banks' (Knight et al. 1933: 5). The Chicago scholars wanted to prohibit the recurrence of the banking crisis caused through the overextension of money creation by the banks against reserves held. They saw the subsequent reduction in the circulating media as the primary cause of the economic crisis of the time. Fisher had a similar belief as did according to Leeson (2003), Frederick Soddy,[37] the 1921 Nobel Laureate in Chemistry who 'considered Fisher's 100% money plan as practically identical to his own' (Leeson 2003: 11). All believed that individuals' behaviours with respect to the medium of exchange has important economic effects. For example, as George Tolley wrote in Yeager (1962) as the public's level of concern rose due to the stock market collapse of 1929, it began to hold money in the form of notes and coin. This led to a reduction of bank reserves and in turn to a reduction in the available money supply. In a self-fulfilling cycle banks were forced to sell assets in a falling market to raise more reserves to meet more deposit withdrawals.[38]

James Tobin (1987: 169) wrote: 'Bank runs in the Depression were an economy wide catastrophe because they became a general run of depositors to currency'. Since banks were carrying only a fraction of reserves to deposits (see Table 3.2.1 above), it was unavoidable that the money supply would contract leading to depressed economic activity.[39] The Federal Reserve did not act as was reasonably expected to and add the required reserves[40] to boost bank lending and thus deposits and the money supply. As Milton Friedman, in reference to the 1929 to 1933 financial crisis wrote in Yeager (1962: 235): 'Without doubt, the most serious mistake in the history of the Reserve System was its mismanagement of monetary matters during those years.'[41] The 1929-33 experience led to economists Knight, Simons and others from Chicago, along with Fisher from Yale, Currie from Harvard and many more, to be convinced 'that structural reorganization was needed to permit better control of the money supply.' (Yeager 1962: 278). These, and other proposals to fix the financial catastrophe of the early 1930s shown below, were the arguments put to President Roosevelt early on in his new administration by the proponents of the Chicago Plan.

In the first of various academic documents issued during the 1930s, arguing for a change in the way money was managed in the economy, the Chicago Plan (Knight et. al. 1933) was a plan for monetary reform, with at its core a radical proposal[42] imposing 100% reserves as support for on demand chequing deposits. In essence banks would be obliged to hold in the form of vault cash or deposits with the Federal Reserve Banks, liquidity matching 100% on demand chequing deposits. As Tolley (Yeager 1962) writes academics in the 1930s were highly motivated to seek such reform due to the high number of bank suspensions over the 1930 to 1933 period. Over 9,000 bank suspensions (see Table 3.2.2 above), with large losses to mainly small depositors, had fed a growing fear, which in turn made further suspensions more likely. Due to the fractional reserve banking of the time, a vast amount of money would need to be injected into the banking system to achieve the 100% reserves required. As Hart (1935) wrote:

> the reserve requirements of the bankers against chequing deposits would be raised from the present sum of about $2,000 million to a sum presumably of $20,000 million or so. Accordingly it would be necessary both to multiply the amount of reserve funds in existence and to get the additional funds into the hands of the banks. (Hart 1935: 105)

The required reserves could be achieved through the central bank printing the money required and using it to buy risk assets from the banks to an amount matching deposits.

The Chicago Plan thus argued that the business of banking had to be bifurcated into two distinct and different streams. As already mentioned, a core belief of the Chicago Plan was that if banks had reserves supporting 100% of deposits, then depositors would not be fearful for their money in the case of a bank failure. The contagion between risk assets and customer deposits would be removed and with it the potential for runs on banks. One half of the dichotomy had to be separated from the other, leaving private banks only with the ability to issue loans against capital and long-term savings. As the Chicago Plan memorandum stated:

> The primary objective of these proposals for permanent reform is that of effecting a complete separation, between different classes of corporations, of the Deposit and Lending functions of existing commercial banks. (Knight et.al. 1933: 5)

According to this radical change, banking legislation would be enacted to mandate the incorporation of an institution:

> (a) which alone shall be entitled to accept funds subject to check or to payment on demand; (b) which shall be required to maintain reserves of 100% in lawful money and/or deposits with the Reserve Banks; (c) which shall serve exclusively as institutions for deposits and transfer of funds; (Knight et.al. 1933: 4)

Furthermore, additional legislation was to be passed providing for the additional:

> incorporation of a distinct class of institutions, in the general form of investment trusts, and subject to government regulation and examination, which institutions shall perform the functions of existing banks with respect to savings deposits; (Knight et.al. 1933: 4)

Fisher described in *100% Money* (1936) how he believed the dismantling of the savings from the lending process should work:

1) the Government, through a specially created authority which Fisher refers to as the "Currency Commission"[43] would monetise enough of the bank's earning assets to generate a liquid position within the bank to match on demand deposits by 100%.

2) this addition of cash by the Currency Commission would not impact the overall money supply since the new money would match deposits.

3) after this initial transfer had occurred, the bank would be mandated to maintain permanently a cash reserve of 100% of customer on demand deposits. In other words, customer cheque deposits would be actual cash deposits held by the bank on behalf of the customer.

4) the bank would be divided into two entities - one to solely act as a custodian and administrator for the customer cheque deposits. The income foregone as a result of the removal of risk assets would be reimbursed through the charging of fees to manage these accounts. There would be no interest payable on the deposit holdings.

5) longer term deposits, or savings as Fisher calls them, would be treated entirely different to on demand deposits. Savings would be "invested" in the second bank entity to spin out of this process. They would bear interest and would be at risk. Thus, the new entity could fund its earning assets from these savings plus capital and retained earnings. This trading bank could also borrow in its own name to lend to clients.

Since the Government, or its appointed entity would inject the required cash into the banking system by purchasing its risk assets, and a large part of those risk assets would be Government bonds, a large part of the government's interest-bearing debt would be reduced. It would be cancelled out as part of the asset/liquidity swap (Fisher 1936). Both the sharp creation and the sharp destruction of the circulating media would be prevented except through the direct actions of the central monetary authority (Hart 1935). Sharp reductions in cash and cheque deposits had the potential to lead to a deflationary spiral with debilitating economic and social consequences as witnessed over the 1929 to 1933 period.[44] Table 3.2.1 shows the money supply[45] falling by nearly 30% over this time.

Commensurate with that the CPI dropped by 25% and GDP by more than 45%. The blame for these economic collapses was laid squarely at the feet of the reduction in circulating media.

How the circulating media (money supply) is determined proved to be a major point of difference between the Chicago Plan and Fisher's 100% Money. Simons, who was heavily influenced by the failure of the British banking Act of 1844,[46] wanted to ensure that there was no 'leakage' of liquidity from on demand checking accounts through banks devising other means of short term almost cash-like instruments. For example, as Philips (1995: 90) quotes Simons in a letter to Fisher:

> Little would be gained by putting demand deposit banking on a 100% basis, if that change were accompanied by increasing disposition to hold, and increasing facilities for holding, liquid "cash" reserves in the form of time-deposits.

Fisher did not see savings deposits as being as liquid or as turning over as often as Simons feared. For Fisher these longer-term fixed deposits need not be included in the money supply and so need not be 100% supported by reserves. As he wrote back to Simons:

> When I see you we can iron this out further perhaps but I have not seen anything in any of your statements so far which would seem to me to justify your fears in regard to savings accounts (Fisher to Simons, December 14, 1934, Fisher Papers, as quoted in Philips 1995: 92).

The question as to how money is defined was, and is, therefore critical when considering the effectiveness of either proposal or its impact on how banking should function (Demeulemeester 2018). Under the Fisher 100% Money proposal banks would be free to continue with fractional reserve banking if the liabilities they generated to fund their loans were not included in the circulating media of exchange. In other words:

> '[u]nder the Currie–Fisher approach, 100% money would spell the end of fractional-reserve money, but not of fractional-reserve banking' (Demeulemeester 2018: 382).

That is, the liabilities would have a longer-term structure than 'on demand'. The Chicago Plan had a more extreme view of banks' liability generating capabilities and their immersion into the media of exchange. Under that Plan 100% money implied an end to not only fractional reserve money but also banking as a means of money creation. The Chicago Plan aimed to abolish banks as 'lending institutions working with savings deposits and replace them with investment trusts working with equity shares' (Demeulemeester 2018: 382). The confusion around this definition, due perhaps to the debate around monetary reform emanating from the 1930s focusing on the extremes of the Chicago Plan, more than Fisher's 100% Money theory, may in fact help to explain why neither proposal was fully taken up (Demeulemeester 2018: 383).

There were other monetary and fiscal measures proposed by the Chicago Plan but for our purposes we consider '[t]he fundamental feature of all the 100 per cent proposals, and the one of greatest importance, is the proposed transformation of the character of our present currency and checking deposits' (Angell 1935: 8). James Angell, who served in the economics faculty of Columbia university from 1924 to 1966, was not however convinced of all aspects of Fisher's '100% Money' proposals. As much as he supported the 100% reserves proposals he was not convinced of the practicality of their application. In his 1935 paper *The 100 Percent Reserve Plan* Angell raises the issues that:

1) if banks were required to sell their government bonds to Fisher's 'Currency Commission' to raise cash in support of

on-demand deposits, then the savings of longer-term investors with the banks would be compromised since the banks would be left holding 'weaker' assets safeguarding those longer-term liabilities. Banks did not qualify their risk assets against on demand or longer-term savings, so they would not be able to differentiate as to which to sell to the Currency Commission.

2) therefore, depositors on hearing rumours of the above asset transfers, would rush to convert all time deposits to on demand or to cash. This had the potential to create the very conditions the Commission was trying to avoid since banks would be forced to sell assets en masse to meet liability requirements.

3) Angell also felt that Fisher had vastly underestimated the total number of assets that the Commission would have to buy from banks to meet the 100% reserves condition. Instead of the ten billion dollars suggested by Fisher, Angell believed something like twenty-six billion would have to be purchased. This amount outstripped the amount of government bonds on issue meaning the Commission would need to buy other assets as well.

Angell also wrote that the methods proposed by Fisher to compensate the banks for the loss of income because of the new arrangements were not feasible and that the concept the government debt could be relieved through the purchase of issued bonds was misleading. Finally, according to Angell there were also legal and constitutional issues, which would act to impede the Currency Commission's goals.[48] All in all however Angell believed that:

> [t]he installation of a 100 per cent reserve system, if it could be successfully accomplished, would give full protection to the holders of the demand liabilities of the banks. Bank runs would cease, bank failures would not alter the volume of demand deposits, and changes in the total quantity of circulating money caused by the effective relending of such

deposits would disappear (Angell 1935: 16).

The application of such a concept however was extremely difficult. Even the Chicago Plan scholars were not unanimous in its application. To them the 100%RB concept could be accomplished but it was the longer-term management of the currency that posed problems for them. As Knight wrote in the 1933 Memorandum:

> Within our group, there are slight differences of opinion as to what constitutes the most desirable policy. Some of us favor a stabilizing of the total quantity of circulating media; some, a stabilizing of total "circulation" ("MV") per period; some favor more complex formulas (e.g., stabilizing per-capita "circulation"). (Knight et al., 1933: 7).

The crux of the matter though being that depositors' savings should be protected from the risk taking and money-making activities of the bank. Next, we investigate why our three economists felt that this was such an important issue to take up.

3.3: The Chicago Plan - Philosophical Groundings for Change

3.3.1: Henry C. Simons (1899-1946)

Henry Calvert Simons was born in Virden, Illinois on October 9, 1899. He died in Chicago Illinois on June 19, 1946. He lectured in economics at the University of Chicago from 1927 until his death in 1946. Simons considered himself a libertarian who was seen as 'a reactionary by professional leftists and a dangerous radical by some conservatives' (Davenport 1946: 5). '"Those who hope for dictatorship,"' Davenport (1946: 6) quotes Simons as saying, '"whether under proletarian or fascist symbols, may rather fittingly refer to us as the impractical visionaries."' Simons believed in true freedom for the markets. Freedom, not just from government, but also from the monopolising power of large corporations. In fact, he was against any centralised institution powerful enough to control the market. He understood however, that to obtain this true freedom for the individual through a free market interaction, that state intervention was required to set the boundaries within which this game could be played. Capitalism, according to Simons, could not exist without the state (Davenport 1946; Simons 1936).

For Simons, (as well as Knight, as will be seen later), laissez faire did not infer complete ignorance of the markets by the state. Again, Davenport quotes Simons:

> "[i]t is an obvious responsibility of the state under this policy to maintain the kind of legal and institutional framework within which competition can function effectively as an agency of control." (Davenport 1946: 6).

The main thrust of Simons' argument was that the state should do both, maintain a strong antitrust posture and an effective monetary policy to obviate the boom and bust cycle. He therefore saw that the so-called end of capitalism being called during the Great Depression was really a failure of government to ensure that the game was played by the rules. Milton Friedman, who saw Simons as a mentor and a 'shaper of his ideas' (Friedman 1967: 1) agreed with Simons' arguments on monetary theory but strongly disagreed with Simons on the subject of monetary reform. Friedman explains in his Henry Simons Lecture given in 1967 that Simons, who wrote about money during the period 1933 to 1945, had to write at a time 'when, thanks to the Keynesian Revolution, the profession came to regard money-in the sense of currency, deposits, banking, and allied issues-as an unimportant and uninteresting subject' (Friedman 1967: 2).

Simons wrote his 'Rules Versus Authorities in Monetary Policy' in 1936. As the true libertarian that he was, he saw the world around him, his beliefs in true liberty and pure market freedom, as being challenged by capitalism (Simons 1936). This dichotomy in belief systems led to his view that capitalism would best survive if it were curtailed, governed, with a given set of strict parameters - as he called them, 'the rules of the game'. He believed that since the mid 19th century banking and monetary practices had evolved that were not conducive to true libertarian freedom. Simons essentially argued that the banking school way of things had gone out of control. His was a currency school belief that implied a limit and control over the capacity for commercial banks to create money through credit. He was however not convinced that a fixed quantity of money was the answer. As he said:

> The fixing of the quantity of circulating media might merely serve to increase the perverse variability in the amounts of "near-moneys" and in the degree of their general acceptability, just as the restrictions on the issue of bank notes presumably served to hasten the development of deposit (checking-account) banking. (Simons 1936: 5)

From the mid 19th century banks had evolved into institutions that had inherited great prerogatives from government. This, according to Simons, allowed them to create obligations that became 'the established medium of payment' (Simons 1936: 9). Along with this came great responsibility, a responsibility however that failed, according to the character development of the profit seeking banking institution that will 'flood the economy with money-substitutes during booms and precipitate futile efforts at general liquidation afterwards' (Simons 1936: 10). The problem as Simons saw it was that banks engaged in leverage that was too high on the support of unsecured assets. This prancing along the minefield meant that too easily a bank might find itself with liquidity problems. The slightest downturn in the markets would cause the banks to attempt to improve their assets and so the spiral of money supply reduction begins. Simons' solution, as stated above was too radical for Friedman. Simons proposed the abolition of banking, as it existed. The creation of short term on demand obligations was the source of the liquidity mismatch that led to the harmful boom bust economic cycles. Simons in effect wanted to see the establishment of 'Savings banks [which] would be transformed into strictly mutual institutions or investment trusts' (Simons 1936: 16).

Another important connection that Simons made during his time in Chicago deserves mention. That is, the connection with the institutionalist and later post-Keynesian student, Hyman Minsky (Whalen 1988: 533). Minsky himself said:

> [t]he fundamentals of a theory of financial instability can be derived from Keynes's General Theory, Irving Fisher's description of a debt deflation, and the writings of Henry Simons' (Minsky 1986: 192).

This is an important connection because Simons, who as already noted was a classical liberal free marketeer, was placed in a common junction with Keynes, the traditional interventionist. In a paper written in 1964, Minsky wrote that it was commonplace to accept that exogenous events were the cause of market turbulence and depression. However, as he saw it endogenous fragilities led to instability, and that 'the evidence that money is a significant part of the mechanism generating a deep depression is strong '(Minsky 1964: 324)'. As a student of Simons in Chicago, Minsky developed his theory on financial instability around a central point of Simons': '[t]he central role of the money supply in past deep depressions is due to the institutional accident that commercial banks were the dominant financial intermediary' (Minsky 1964: 326). This was Simons' proposal via the Chicago Plan, to remove this potential source of economic instability and allow a true capitalism to develop.

Here we come to the crux of the matter regarding Simons' contribution to the Chicago Plan. It was his belief that in certain matters private commercial enterprise could not, under the governance of competition, provide the best possible service for the community. Monopoly conditions led to 'extreme inequality of power' (Simons 1948: 52). Whilst he believed that central planning was a 'mongrel system' (Simons 1948: 52), he also saw that the vast inequality of power and wealth attributed to the giant corporation through lax regulation as 'one of the greatest sins of governments against the free-enterprise system'(Simons 1948: 52). He did not believe however that in these circumstances overly regulatory conditions would solve the issue. He quite simply believed that the government should take full ownership of the enterprise in question and govern it in the public good. He wrote:

> *In general, however, the state should face the necessity of actually taking over, owning, and managing directly, both the railroads and utilities, and all other industries in which it is impossible to maintain effectively competitive conditions.* (Simons 1948: 51 italics in the original).

Knut Wicksell the Swedish economist pre-empted Simons on this point having written in 1898 that:

> the banks' prime duty is not to earn a great deal of money but to provide the public with a medium of exchange—and to provide this medium in adequate measure, to aim at stability of prices. In any case, their obligations to society are enormously more important than their private obligations, and if they are ultimately unable to fulfil their obligations to society along the lines of private enterprise—which I very much doubt—then they would provide a worthy activity for the State. (Wicksell 1936: 190)

Simons' reasoning along these lines follows a natural path to that of monetary policy. He poses the proposition that a government monetary policy of wanton increases, followed by precipitous decreases, in money supply would be economically disastrous (Simons 1948). That is exactly the condition that existed, he continues, but not on the part of government, rather on the part of the commercial banking enterprise. Banks had been given the freedom by lax government controls, to 'usurp…the basic state function of providing the medium of circulation (and of private "cash" reserves)' (Simons 1948: 54). Simons wrote this essay in 1934,[49] just at the trough of the great Depression. His statement that '[i]t is no exaggeration to say that the major proximate factor in the present crisis is commercial banking' (Simons 1948: 54) anchors the debate running through this essay between the currency school and the banking school way of doing things. He believed that the monopoly power given to banks in creating the medium of exchange was a crucial factor in increasing the 'economic loss and human misery accompanying a given deflation' (Simons 1948: 54). Further, any such deflation would be far more prolonged than necessary. In the end however, Simons did not blame the banks or capitalism. He blamed the state for providing the freedom to the banks to act the way they did:

> Laissez faire, to repeat, implies a division of tasks between competitive and political controls; and the failure of the system, if it has failed, is properly to be regarded as a result of failure of the state, especially with respect to money, to do its part. (Simons 1948: 55)

3.3.2: Frank Hyneman Knight (1885-1972)

Quite a lot is lost in the translation from the actual event to the written word. This is even more so when writing many years after the event. If today the memories of the stock market crash and its aftermath during the period of the Great Recession from mid 2007 to early 2009 are already dimming with the passage of time, what do we understand of the great stock market crash of 1929 and the Great Depression that followed? To understand the motivations of free marketeers such as Frank Knight to increase government oversight over the banks and the markets, it is necessary to understand the trauma and cyclonic noise being caused at the time by the collapsing financial world. J.K. Galbraith's account 'The Great Crash of 1929' (1954) goes very close to setting the scene under which Knight, and other Chicago monetarists, propounded their theories on changing the mechanics of a financial infrastructure that had evolved over the past 100 years. One can only pretend to understand the fear that this financial maelstrom must have imposed on all - from the poorest unemployed to the newly incumbent President Roosevelt. Something must have gone wrong to allow this to occur, but as already mentioned above, it was not capitalism that had died, it was government regulation that had lapsed.

Frank Knight joined the university of Chicago in 1927 and stayed, teaching throughout his career until he retired in 1957. Up until his death in 1972 Knight remained active within the Chicago School community (Cowan 2016, Emmett 2009). As a teacher he was possessed with 'a hard-nosed, often entertaining skepticism' (Formaini 2002: np) and he 'saw his vocation, in part, as that of disturbing the easy epistemological assumptions of his fellow-economists' (Emmett 2009: XXVII). Yet he was renowned for his insights and deeply influenced many of his pupils; four of whom went on to earn the Nobel Prize for Economics (Milton Friedman, George Stigler, James Buchanan and Paul Samuelson). Unlike Keynes who rose to true eminence as an economist, Knight was more renowned as a teacher and for 'bringing to light the true economic significance of risk' (Cowan 2016: 3). Knight was an original author of the Chicago Plan memorandum (Knight et al. 1933) but his further contributions to the development of the arguments for a 100% Reserve system seem to fade behind those of Simons and Fisher. The fact that an influential, classical, liberal free marketeer such as Frank Knight would conceive that government-imposed currency rules upon banks, to forbid them from the practice of fractional reserve banking, would resolve the deeply distressing impacts of artificially created business cycles, added great credence to the arguments of the time for monetary reform.

Knight's preoccupation with the impact that commercial banking had on the money supply predates the Chicago Plan of 1933.[50] There were two short contributions by him that highlight this, and both were written in 1927. Firstly, there was a contribution by him to a discussion piece (Fisher et al. 1927) regarding the interest rate theory of Professor Frank Fetter from Princeton University.[51] In this March 1927 article Knight clearly outlines his concern with fractional reserve banking. He writes that commercial banking can be split into its two functions - that of intermediating between savers and investors for the supply of capital on the one hand and the creation of the media of exchange on the other. However, he is not happy with the arrangement since he feels that banks have too much influence on the capital markets because of their monopoly over the creation of the money supply. Knight describes how the capital available to investors is created largely through the issuance of loans by the banks - and for this 'service'[52] of increasing the medium of exchange banks get to charge a fee in the form of interest. This interest rate then impacts all other interest rates in the capital market. He felt, years before the Chicago Plan came into play 'that the whole problem of the relation of commercial banking to the capital market is crying loudly for thorough examination' (Fisher et al., 1927: 121).

The next instance we get of Knight's concerns with commercial banking's power to increase (and decrease) the money supply comes just a month later in April 1927 with his review of Frederick

Soddy's book *Wealth, Virtual Wealth and Debt* (Soddy 1933 (1926). Soddy's expertise in the world of physics and chemistry was undeniable, as his 1921 Nobel Prize in Chemistry attested to; however, his foray into the world of economics often labelled him as a crank.[53] Soddy wrote about the flaws in money and banking because of its detrimental impact on society and highlighting the inequality that evolved because of it. He emphasised the differences between real wealth and 'virtual wealth' (money).[54] In his review[55] of Soddy's book (Knight 1927) Knight critically wrote:

> The practical thesis of the book is distinctly unorthodox, but is in our opinion both highly significant and theoretically correct. In the abstract, it is absurd and monstrous for society to pay the commercial banking system "interest" for multiplying several fold the quantity of medium of exchange when (a) a public agency could do it at negligible cost, (b) there is no sense in having it done at all, since the effect is simply to raise the price level, and (c) important evils result, notably the frightful instability of the whole economic system and its periodical collapse in crises, which are in large measure bound up with the variability and uncertainty of the credit structure if not directly the effect of it. (Knight 1927: 732)

Knight's burgeoning thoughts[56] on the impact that commercial banking could have on the broader economy, through its monopoly powers to increase and decrease the media of exchange were further solidified over the subsequent few years because of the price action which led to the Crash of '29 and the subsequent Great Depression.

As a classical liberal, Knight was fully aware of the value of developing a science of economics and price theory through its mathematisation. He was also aware of the value of commercial banking in sourcing the capital that was necessary for the development of a burgeoning industrial economy. Knight nevertheless agreed with Soddy's proposals to transform the way the media of exchange was created. Knight believed the existing monetary arrangement was the wrong organisation for a democratic, liberal society and wrote about 100% reserves banking in the two 1933 Chicago Plan memoranda (March and November 1933), but did not write about the topic again until he raised it in *Intelligence and Democratic Action*, (1960). In the first of a series of six lectures given at the University of Virginia in 1958, Knight refers to the stupidity of 'the idea and policy of creating wealth or prosperity by making money abundant and cheap'[57] (1960: 5) and importantly (concerning a continuing connection with Soddy) 'the "money illusion," confusing money with real wealth' (1960: 7). Further in this piece, Knight however repudiates the idea that through technological advancement humanity should be able to improve its lot. He refers to this as "scientificism," the notion that social problems can be solved by applying the methods by which man has achieved increasing mastery over nature (1960: 11). This was a critical difference to Soddy's argument. Knight approaches this thought through 'value problems, to which natural science has little relevance' (1960: 11), i.e., the Chicagoan price theory. The kernel of Knight's theory being that technological advancement may well provide advantages and power, but it doesn't say how that power is to be allocated and used. Those decisions are made through the assignment of value.

A reading of Knight's *Intelligence and Democratic Action* (1960) however may give the reader reason to question what Knight's tale has to do with economics at all. This collection of lectures did not elaborate on the maths or neoclassical abstractions of the economics of the times. There were however lots of connections to humanity and its true considerations. Knight talks about people and how they truly behave. He considers and ponders human nature. As Van Horn & Emmett (2015: 1445) write about Knight:

> But the liberal revolution had several flaws in Knight's estimation. It over-estimated the ability of markets to constrain concentrations of economic power and under-estimated the potential for economic concentration to be wedded to political power. It over-estimated individual responsibility in the absence of common moral foundations and under-estimated the rent-seeking potential in democracy.

And: 'Knight argued that these flaws revealed liberalism's failed understanding of human nature' (ibid). By the time knight gave those lectures the rising tide of neoclassical economics, in combination with Keynesian[58] solutions to the problems of employment and aggregate demand, had swamped Knight's influence over the Chicago School because of 'his emphasis on democratic discussion and ethics' (Van Horn & Emmett 2015: 1444).[59] It had already drowned Soddy's attempts to raise awareness of the pitfalls of the contemporary monetary arrangements in the first half of the twentieth century.

In his 1927 review of Soddy's book Knight uses the term 'evil' to describe the influence of commercial banking on the money supply through the issue of credit. He uses a similar term in his 1958 lectures in the same reference:

> Commercial banking is a device that might have been invented by the devil for multiplying all these bad effects, but we still have it in spite of the fact that some eminent economists have advocated 100 per cent bank reserves (Knight 1960: 104).

One was used in 1927, the other in 1958. Knight had not forgotten nor changed his view on the impact that commercial banking has on society through its power to coin the media of exchange. It seems that Knight considered the creation of money through the issuance of debt by commercial banks as 'malum per se'[60]. Knight continues in the same article however to voice the concern that has plagued the various proposals for 100% reserves banking. He wrote: '[h]owever if we got rid of fractional reserve banking, it would not be any guarantee against general expansion and contraction of the money circulation' (Knight 1960: 104). This concern was a perennial issue for the currency school advocates dating from the failure of the 1844 British Banking Act to prohibit banks from creating alternative means of liquidity.[61] Knight, in the same article then answers his own question by suggesting it can only be a government solution: 'The evils of the economic order must be dealt with, if at all, by the government—that organization or agency by which a society acts as a unit, or simply by which a society acts' (Knight 1960: 104). This is a connection to the sovereign money proposals to be discussed in chapter 6. But first let's see what Fisher had to say about all of this.

3.3.3: Irving Fisher (1867-1947)

Turning to Yale, the brilliant Irving Fisher was the more practical man, providing us with the tools, the nuts and bolts of an understanding of the monetary equation, debt deflation and banking. Bordo & Rockoff (2011: 39) writing about Fisher's take up of the Chicago Plan crusade write about his contributing to the debate by "absorbing the thinking of his fellow economists and then packaging these radical sounding ideas in a form that would persuade the public". Fisher was able to clearly describe, propose and put his arguments in a manner which has made him one to whom much of today's neoclassical theory is owed (Tobin 2005). Bordo & Rockoff (2011) provide an excellent summary of Fisher's major contributions to economics. They write about Fisher's foundational work regarding the quantity theory of money, the Fisher effect, Gibson's Paradox, business cycles and the Phillips Curve. Further they discuss Fisher's various schemes for monetary reform in the shape of the compensated dollar, a mandate for price stability, 100% money and stamped money. Conjoining all these works is Fisher's ultimate preoccupation with the stability of the media of exchange. He wrote in the introduction to his 1912 *How to Invest When Prices Are Rising* (Fisher et al.) about the impact of deflation and inflation on investments. The servant, he wrote, who invested $100 fifteen years ago receives $50 on her investment - but on maturity she finds that her $150 today barely buys what $100 would have bought 15 years ago - she went without her $100 for fifteen years for nothing![62] The other side of the instability coin arises when money gains in value through debt deflation leading to economic crisis and depression.

The asset price deflation that occurred as a consequence of the stock market crash of 1929 reduced Fisher's 10 million net worth by 11 million (Dimand 2005).[63] This served to concentrate Fisher's analysis as he sought to explain why the Crash of 1929 led to such a deep and prolonged debt-deflation, when compared to say the strong recovery from the 1920-21 crash. As Dimand (2005: 190) writes Keynes did not appear too pre-occupied with the debt-deflation process in the General Theory (1936) however Fisher saw it as a core issue to explain the great depression. We explore Fisher's thoughts through two of his writings: The Debt-Deflation Theory of Great Depressions (1933) and 100% Money (1936).

1. The Debt-Deflation Theory of Great Depressions (1933)

Fisher starts by detailing the large diversity of an economy and the difficulty that such a system has in maintaining equilibrium based on the forces of supply and demand. As Fisher says only 'in the imagination can all of these variables remain constant and be kept in equilibrium by the balanced forces of human desires' (Fisher 1933: 337). He continues that the study of economics consists of two components - a) the study of this imaginary equilibrium and b) the study of the system when it is not in the imaginary state i.e.

when it is in disequilibrium. The former can be constructed through static analysis and the latter is founded on the system's dynamics. That one is imaginary and the other real seems to be what Fisher is telling us. Cycles are not dominated by one particular impulse, which manifests as a trend, lasting until it ends. Rather, Fisher says there are many interwoven economic impulses working their way through and overlapping each other that create, in the net, a directional reaction. Seeking, but never really finding equilibrium; until disequilibrium ensues and a different paradigm takes hold.

As sensible as any of these cycle impulses might be they are relegated as minor in comparison to Fisher's two dominant cycle rulers: "*over-indebtedness* to start with and *deflation* following soon after" (fisher 1933: 341 italics in original). Over-indebtedness[64] resulting from the upswing boom, and deflation coming as a consequence of the downward slump. The extremes of these two "big bad actors" (Fisher 1933: 341), resulting from over-investment and over-speculation as bad as they are already, are further magnified through the use of debt to gain greater risk exposure leverage[65]. As the cycle feeds on itself, gorging on the over-indebted inflated over-speculation, birth is given to over-confidence. These conditions are the extremes that occur from time to time:

> Disturbances in these two factors-debt and the purchasing power of the monetary unit will set up serious disturbances in all, or nearly all, other economic variables. On the other hand, if debt and deflation are absent, other disturbances are powerless to bring on crises comparable in severity to those of 1837, 1873, or 1929-33. (Fisher 1933: 341).

Along with the two 'bad boys' of debt and deflation come seven further linkages which in totality provide Fisher's nine major factors contributing to economic depressions. These nine factors in summary are all from Fisher 1933: 342:

1. *Debt liquidation* leads to *distress selling* and to
2. *Contraction of deposit currency*, as bank loans are paid off, and to a slowing down of velocity of circulation leading to
3. A *fall in the level of prices.* Assuming action to reflate the economy was not taken then there must be
4. *A still greater fall in the net worths of business*, precipitating bankruptcies and
5. *A like fall in profits*, which in a "capitalistic," that is, a private-profit society, leads the concerns which are running at a loss to make
6. A *reduction in output, in trade and in employment* of labor. These losses, bankruptcies, and unemployment, lead to
7. *Pessimism and loss of confidence*, which in turn lead to
8. *Hoarding and slowing down still more the velocity of circulation*
9. The above eight changes cause *complicated disturbances in the rates of interest*, particularly a fall in the nominal, or money, rates and a rise in the real, or commodity, rates of interest.

As prices spiral downwards and holders of debt are forced to sell assets to repay the debt, the downward momentum accelerates. If the amount of debt was great enough to begin with then we have **Fisher's famous paradox of debt**:

> *the very effort of individuals to lessen their burden of debts increases it, because of the mass effect of the stampede to liquidate in swelling each dollar owed.* Then we have the great paradox which, I submit, is the chief secret of most, if not all, great depressions: *The more the debtors pay, the more they owe* (Fisher 1933: 344 italics in the original).

What makes Fisher's debt-deflation theory so compelling is the realism implicit in his consignment of the above nine linkages to human psychology. Shiller (2013) compares this to an early development of behavioural economics. Based around the concepts of human greed and fuelled by the preparedness of bankers to create the required deposits through loans, Fisher (1933) clearly details the eagerness of individuals to go into debt in anticipation of future gains. Soddy (1933: 83) also alluded to the compelling force of human psychology when he wrote that debt is created through 'the mere consent of two minds. By the mere fiat of the Human Will'. Frank Knight in his caustic review of Keynes' General Theory stated that 'speculative psychology tends to give rise to a kind of momentum or cumulative tendency in price changes' (Knight 1937: 123 n. 24). What drives this creation of an obligation on behalf of some to others is described by Fisher (1933: 349) as:

> (a) the lure of big prospective dividends or gains in income in the remote future; (b) the hope of selling at a profit, and realizing a capital gain in the immediate future; (c) the vogue of reckless promotions, taking advantage of the habituation of the public to great expectations; (d) the development of downright fraud, imposing on a public which had grown credulous and gullible.

All of this leads to an understanding that as we have already seen, capitalism cannot function without the growth in debt as reflected by an increasing money supply.[66]

2. 100% Money (1936)

The aim of his relatively small book was immensely large. Fisher wanted to re-establish the historic 100% system of banking. As he wrote, he wanted to revert to 'the conservative safety-deposit system of the old goldsmiths, before they began lending out improperly what was entrusted to them for safekeeping' (Fisher 1936: 19). Deposits with banks would remain wholly within their accounts and not be lent out to others. The current 10% system of Fisher's day had to be re-adjusted back to 100% reserves to support deposits fully. Such an act:

> would effectually restrain the monetary inflation and deflation incident to our present system; that is, would actually stop the irresponsible creation and destruction of circulating medium by our thousands of commercial banks which now act like so many private mints. (Fisher 1936 xi)

As Fisher saw it the only way that the medium of exchange can enter the system is when someone goes into debt. That can be an individual, a business or the government. The paradox lies in the fact that just when circulating media is most needed in order to stimulate demand, that people are the least inclined to go into debt in order to create it.[67] 'Such must often be our predicament so long as we have a system under which our circulating medium is a by-product of private debt' (Fisher 1936: 105). Keynes however, who also wrote about money in 1936, did not believe that 'new money' was necessarily required to generate increased aggregate demand. Keynes believed that consumption could increase over income through an increase in money velocity or through drawing down on reserves.[68] Regardless of Keynes, the more than 30% reduction in the money supply led to a large economic contraction that in the final analysis, only the government could help to supplant through additional government fiscal deficits, funded through borrowing.[69]

Keynes in fact was not a supporter of Fisher's 100% plan. This was demonstrated some eight years later when during his attendance at the Bretton Woods conference in 1944 Fisher wrote to Keynes, head of the English delegation, promoting his 100% reserves money plan:

> I think it quite possible it could, after the war, be put over for Americans and other countries, as the best national plan to interlock with the international plan you are now trying to put over. We could then avoid great inflation and deflation in future over a wide area. (Fisher to Keynes July 4 1944 quoted in Allen 1993: 715 n49)

Keynes however remained unconvinced writing Fisher:

> In my judgment deflation is in the near future a much more dangerous risk than inflation. I am afraid of your formula because I think it would, certainly in England, have a highly deflationary suggestion to a great many people. Apart from that, I am satisfied that in British conditions anyhow ... we can obtain complete control over the quantity of money by means much less capable of exciting unfavourable comment and opposition. (Letter from Keynes to Fisher, July 7 1944, quoted in Allen 1993: 715 n49).

Comparison to Keynes is inserted here because his General Theory eclipsed Fisher and the Chicago plan for the next four decades, before Friedman (1960) from Chicago and Tobin (1985) from Yale refreshed Fisher's thinking. Fisher in his typical sequential style developed in the *Purchasing Power of Money* (1922) further evidence that movements in the supply of money impacted movements in prices. In his 1933 Debt-Deflation Theory Fisher showed how unanticipated movements in prices on the real value of nominal debt impacted human psychology leading to downward panics, after the upwards euphoria. With these works Fisher had already laid the foundation for his (1936) *100% Money* where he put forward the Chicagoan 100% reserves arguments forcibly. That is, if banks were prohibited from expanding the money supply in boom periods, and then contracting it during the inevitable downward corrections, then the pain and hardships of depressions would be avoided. The 'knight errant's' (Allen 1993: 709) determination to persuade those in power to install policies aimed at removing the disastrous boom bust cycles caused through fluctuations in the money supply continued until his death in 1947. And they are continuing still.

3.4 The Chicago Plan - Policy Outcomes

Major economic or political reforms do not just occur spontaneously. They occur because of a crisis (Papadimitriou 1996). President Roosevelt certainly was responding to a crisis that gave him an opportunity, under the auspices of the New Deal, to dramatically change banking practices. That is, to divide and separate the functions of banking between money creation and intermediating between savers and borrowers. The policy changes that occurred subsequently however, fell far short of those proposed by a large consensus of academics of the time.[70] To be fair to Roosevelt, he had a large contingency of national financial emergencies to consider from the start (Phillips 1995). The collapse of more than 9,000 banks over the three years to then had destroyed confidence in the banking system. The Pecora Inquiry into banking practices and securities dealings had further undermined confidence in the American financial system through its discoveries of great abuses by the country's top financiers (Papadimitriou 1996). Adding to these confidence sapping calamities Roosevelt's first act on taking office on 4 March 1933 was to declare a national banking holiday for the period 4-9 March. As Richard Sylla writes (Papadimitriou 1996: 15) the events in the month leading to Roosevelt's inauguration 'serves to remind us that all the pillars of the US financial system were then collapsing'.

Into this financial maelstrom the Chicago Plan was introduced to the Roosevelt administration. In a flurry of activity over its first 100 days Roosevelt passed various acts addressing the economic situation - especially the banking and agricultural crises. Some of the important Acts passed were:

1) The American Banking Act 9 March 1933. Passed in a day of chaos in Congress, it allowed twelve Federal Reserve Banks to meet the call for funds by banks on their re-opening after the Bank Holiday. The FRBs would discount good assets in exchange for funds and thus guarantee that banks would be able to meet deposit withdrawals.
2) Executive Order 6102 5 April 1933 criminalising the possession of gold by private individuals and corporations
3) April 19, 1933, the U.S. went off the gold standard.
4) May 1933 the Agricultural Adjustment Act (AAA). An amendment to the AAA gave the President the power to issue greenbacks and to monetise gold. This was an important power that Roosevelt could have used to mandate 100% reserves banking and never did.
5) The Banking Act of 1933 passed in June 1933. Otherwise known as the Glass-Stegall Act, it separated investment and commercial banking. This Act also created Federal Deposit Insurance through the FDIC and created the Federal Open Market Committee with one member from each Federal district.

Senator Bronson Cutting from New Mexico received a copy of the November 1933 Chicago Memorandum and became a staunch champion of 100% reserves banking with the government reclaiming its constitutional powers to be the sole coiner of the medium of exchange. Henry Simons met with Senator Cutting in March 1934 to discuss the drafting of a bill to enable these reforms (Phillips 1992, Laina 2015). In various discussions seeking support for the Bill Cutting wrote:

> The fight against the abolition of the credit power of private banks will be a savage one, for their power as a unit is without equal in the country. Knowing this is why I think back to the events of March 4, 1933, with a s'ick heart. For then, with even the bankers thinking the whole economic system had crashed to ruin, the nationalization of banks by President Roosevelt could have been accomplished without a word of protest. It was President Roosevelt's great mistake. Now the bankers will make a mighty struggle [Cutting 1934: 121, quoted in Phillips 1992: 20).

In Cutting's view, banks could still operate as private institutions as long as they held 100% reserves against deposits, but they would not be allowed to 'create' credit.

Senator Cutting's Bill gained momentum in government through early 1935. With his untimely death in an airplane crash in May 1935 however the Bill lost its momentum and failed to proceed. It did serve a purpose in that it was seen as the radical version of banking reforms as proposed by the Chicago Plan. As Philips (1992: 35) quotes: "Compared with the 100 per cent reserve plan, it will be seen, the banking act of 1935 is weak tea" (Tribune on February 25, 1935, p. 411). Against the possibility of the Cutting Bill passing, Roosevelt's Banking Act 1935 reforms were seen as acceptable reforms. Even though the core proposal of the Chicago Plan was not implemented it did have an impact on the New Deal legislation with the Banking Acts of 1933 and 1935 giving the government better control of monetary policy. Fisher maintained his lobbying for 100% banking, writing numerous letters to Roosevelt over the years and receiving what appear to be stonewalling replies in return (Allen 1993). Roosevelt had not obviously supported the Chicago Plan at any stage, and he was vehemently opposed to

Bronson Cutting and therefore did not support his Bill. What was motivating, or in fact holding back Roosevelt from passing the legislation for 100% reserves banking?[73] Allen gives an opinion on this when he writes regarding Fisher:

> But he wrote his son in early 1935 that, while "Congress is ready" to accept the 100 per cent reserve idea, "the President is afraid of the bankers (Allen 1993: 710).

Carol Quigley, in his magnum opus Tragedy and Hope (1966) provides an alternative insight into why the Chicago Plan reforms did not pass legislation. Writing about Roosevelt he says that the President had certainly grasped the fact that a:

> lack of purchasing power was the cause of the lack of demand which made unsold goods and unemployment, but he had no idea of the causes of the depression and had quite orthodox ideas on the nature of money (Quigley 1966: 534).

Therefore, Roosevelt was prepared to act in an unorthodox manner regarding the budget deficits required to relieve the stress of the period, but the New Deal itself was financially orthodox in its orientation towards money. Roosevelt just simply borrowed the money from the private banks to fund his deficit spending. The New Deal 'allowed the bankers to create the money, (*the administration*) borrowed it from the banks, and spent it' (Quigley 1966: 534). As a result, Roosevelt treated the symptoms of the depression rather than the causes, which was the exact opposite of what the Chicago Plan postulated should be done. In fact, for the twelve years that he was in power Roosevelt, under the authority of the Agricultural Act passed in 1933, had the statutory ability to by-pass the banks and issue fiat money in the form of greenbacks to fund his deficit. Something he never did.

In the end, the net result of all the activism by academics of the Chicago School and beyond failed to persuade government to meet the goals required by them for a more just monetary management. These goals were amply set out by Frederick Soddy and quoted by Merricks (1996: 167) in her biography:

> but that until the money system in (sic) re-inverted and restored to its original function as the national instrument for distributing all that can be produced at a constant price level, science will continue to bring not peace and prosperity but frustration, wars and destruction over the whole world.

Robert Hemphill put a similar sentiment in the foreword to Fisher's 1936 book:

> Our statesmen have consistently declined to study this question and provide a sound monetary system, an adequate and permanent currency, scientifically calculated to expand consistently with our increasing population and our increasing ability to produce. (Fisher 1936 (1935): xxiii)]

The currency school argument had met the banking school deterrence.

3.5 Conclusion

Section 3.2 initially showed the extent of the financial crisis of the 1930s and why the system needed change. It then dealt with the proposals for change put forward by the Chicago Plan. The main points put forward by the Chicago Plan for Banking Reform strove to firstly remove the possibility of bank losses from over lending impacting upon the security of customer deposits. This could be done by dismantling the deposit/liquidity function from the risk assets / capital function. Secondly the Federal Reserve Banks had to be nationalised. The government needed to take control of the issuance of the medium of exchange. An added benefit would be that government debt would be dramatically reduced, ultimately reverting to zero. It was important at the same time however to continue to allow the free market to determine the lending prerogatives of banks since that was seen as the ultimate means for the distribution of investment capital. That is, the proposed changes were to be quantitative in nature through the control of the volume of the medium of exchange. The qualitative aspect of banking was to remain with the bankers.

Section 3.3 dealt with the thinking behind the efforts of three prominent American economists to convince policy makers about the need to separate the banking function of money creation from that of bank lending. Simons and Knight from Chicago made the first sortie in 1933 with the presentation of their short monogram, The Chicago Plan, to President Roosevelt. The cause was later taken up with full force by Fisher with his 100% Money; a cause that he promoted until his death in 1947. This section wanted to shine a light on why such classical laissez faire believers in the free market were insisting on such extreme state action to curb the power of the banking industry. These three economists were part of a substantial cohort essentially making the argument that money should be a creature of the state - not a thing of private markets. It was an argument in refutation of the neoclassical liberalism instituting the responsibility and methodology on the individual and it was an intrusion into a rampant laissez faire that swelled from Adam Smith's classical economics.

Section 3.4 dealt with the outcomes of the Chicago Plan's lobbying for reform. In the end many of its proposed changes were implemented such as deposit guarantees, separation of investment from commercial banking and changes to the Federal Reserve System to give it more powers over monetary policy. However wide and unorthodox the Acts passed in the two New Deal programs were, the funding for them was all done through the orthodox means of borrowing from banks. No doubt there were intractable problems with the implementation of the 100% reserves reforms, some of these being the advent of new technologies developing new and alternate means of payments, as well as the actual transition to the new scheme. Nevertheless, and to leave the final words to this chapter to Phillips:

> If we are ever again faced with economic, and particularly financial, problems on the level of the Great Depression, the clamour for the separation of the depository and lending functions of banks may reappear (Phillips 1992: 45).

Chapter 4

Determination of the Money Supply, the Bank Balance Sheet and the Alford Cross

4.1 Introduction

The establishment of the Federal Reserve System (FED) in December 1913 saw the entrenchment of credit creation banking in the Unites States. The Banking School argument depicted in chapter 2 for a flexible currency and centralised reserves base won through, allowing banks to increase their issuance of the media of exchange through the creation of bank liabilities. In chapter 3 we saw the financial volatility in the late 1920s that led to the Great Depression of the 1930s and the currency school arguments put forward by Knight and Simons from Chicago, and Fisher from Yale, to curb the power of banks to increase and decrease the money supply. Their core argument being that the stability of the money supply was too important to be left in the hand of private corporations such as banks. Therefore, the power to issue money should be divorced from the ability to issue loans. Chapter 4 now looks at the theory underpinning the determination of the money supply and the structural workings of the bank balance sheet, and its expansion under fractional reserves banking. As Hyman Minsky maintained '[a] capitalist economy can be described by a set of interrelated balance sheets and income statements' (Minsky

1992: 12). An understanding of the bank balance sheet will help to explain why an increase in bank lending leads to an increase in deposits and how these 'shifts in the composition of banks' balance sheets have important consequences for our understanding of the source of financial instability' (Jorda et al. 2014: 3).

Since the establishment of the FED banks could either replenish reserves by borrowing from each other or directly from the central bank. Section 4.2 looks at theories of the money supply proposed by Chick (1992) and Goodhart (2017). As we will see, Chick's '5 stages of banking' can be safely combined with Goodhart's '4 approaches in the determination of the money supply'. Section 4.3 will show how bank accounting measures the flow of reserves and deposits, at both the aggregate system and individual bank levels. The logic behind this theoretical exposition being that to understand the two enquiries analysed in this report, the great Depression of the 1930s and the Great Financial Crisis of 2007/09, it will be helpful to understand the monetary processes underpinning the financial system. In fact, as we will see in Section 4.4 the cash and equity components of the bank balance sheet demonstrate the Achilles heel of the capitalist finance system.[74] In this section Roger Alford further develops a simplified and yet extremely effective means to demonstrate how the bank balance sheet actually functions. A difficult and complex topic is transformed into an easily understood one. By using the Alford Cross, developed directly from Alford's technique, we will see how the arguments posed by Simons, Knight and Fisher may have been applied to engender 100% reserves banking. Alford also serves to tie the Chicago Plan attempts at monetary reform to the Sovereign Money efforts after the Great Financial Crisis. As we will see, it is all done with numbers.

4.2: Determination of the Money Supply

The establishment of the Federal Reserve in 1913 also led to the consolidation of clearing arrangements which made the payment through chequing accounts even more acceptable. This saw deposits representing not just savings but transaction balances 'financing the consumption circuit' (Chick 1992: 195). This money, created as deposits through loan issuance by banks, was recycled from bank to bank not leaving the system as a whole to any great extent, but rather would be netted off amongst the banks as reserves transactions within their accounts with the central bank. At the end of the day banks with deficits in their reserves account would borrow reserves from banks holding a surplus. As Chick (1992: 195) says individual banks now felt 'emboldened to lend 'money they haven't got' setting off the multiple expansion for the system as a whole which we now take for granted' (see figure 4.2.3 below for example). Much later Charles Goodhart (2017: 37) further exposes the weakness in the theory that deposits lead to loans. Essentially, as Goodhart writes, under what is now a fairly redundant scenario (still talked about today), a bank would buy an asset and issue a loan with no immediate loss in reserves. That is, because existing deposits fund the new deposit created from the loan. As is now readily accepted however, there is a commensurate drain of reserves on an individual bank making a loan so that by inference the bank needs to fund the loan after the fact since the funds it allocates to the borrower do not come from some other existing source. The bank does not debit an existing account holding the funds and credit these to the recipient of the loan's account. Instead, the bank creates the funds allocated to the borrower by passing a book entry. The balance sheet examples below clearly show this flow of book entries.

As the Board of Governors of the Federal Reserve wrote in 1939:

> It may seem that it ought to be the other way round—that bank loans and investments would be derived from bank deposits instead of bank deposits being derived from loans and investments; and it is true that deposits would not grow out of loans if currency were used by the public for monetary payments to the exclusion of bank deposits transferable by check. But as it is, the public in general prefers to have its monetary funds—including what it borrows—on deposit in banks rather than in the form of currency in its own possession. The result of this preference is that the proceeds of loans go on deposit to be disbursed by check, and aggregate deposits are increased. (FED BG 1939: 39)

Table 4.2.1 below shows a table drawn from Goodhart (2017) and chick (1992). It is useful because there are points to be made regarding the evolution of the creation of the money supply, the deregulation of finance, the financialisation of the broader economy and the preponderous growth in the debt to GDP ratio. The latter points are dealt with in the next chapter but here we acknowledge that the evolution and growth of banking as a proportion of GDP is directly related to the evolution of the growth in the money supply. Furthermore, as we saw during the Columbia (1908) conference lectures, finance was already aware that investments led to savings well before the issue was picked up in the 1930s by economists such as Keynes (1936).

Table 4.2.1 - Money supply theories

MONEY SUPPLY THEORIES			
Theory	*Goodhart 2017: 'Determination of the Money Supply'*	*Chick 1992: Evolution of the Banking System'*	*Comments*
Deposits cause Loans	Passive: banks wait for deposits before creating loans.	Stage 1: Banks are dependant on deposits for reserves and on reserves for lending capacity. **ΔD>ΔR>ΔL**	Changes in Deposits influenced changes in Reserves influenced changes in Loans
Money Base Multiplier	Just vary R/D ratio: CB reserves dominated extent of bank lending.	Stage 2: The 'bank deposit multiplier' is the relevant theory. Banks can lend to a multiple of reserves. **ΔR>ΔL>ΔD**	Two tiered money system: CB money (Tier 1) dictated how much Bank money (Tier 2) there was. Deposits increasingly become means of payment.
Credit Counterparts	Quite passive: Excess demand for funds by borrowers met through bank lending.	Stages 3 and 4: Bank lending is influenced by demand for funds. **ΔLd>ΔL>ΔD>ΔR** L(d) = demand for loans	Banks access required funding via wholesale markets and securitisation. Banks set their own growth agendas. Central Bank influences loans expansion through cost of reserves. Reduces cost to promote expansion and raises cost to contract loan growth.
Loans create Deposits	Dominant: Argument that commercial banks create money supply only partially true. Borrower demand is the real determinant. Sees banks as the 'passive residual providers of finance'.	Banks develop 'liability management' as consequence of greater deregulation and competition. In 1981 formal reserve requirements abolished in the U.K. LoL resort liquidity taken for granted. 'Moral hazard' the only limit to meeting loan demand. **ΔL(s)>ΔL>ΔD>ΔR** L(s) = Loan sales	During the Columbia 1908 Conference Frank Vanderlipp was already describing banking as the business of issuing loans (investments) which led to deposits (savings). The removal of post Depression and WW2 banking regulations creates an environment of competitive free-for-all lending.

Source: Goodhart 2017, Chick 1992

Goodhart's final point in the chart above is that 'banking is a service industry, which sets the terms and conditions whereby the private sector can create additional money for itself' (Goodhart 2017: 33). This is an interesting point that has connotations for the arguments posed by Seligman in 1908 (Columbia 1908) and Knight, Simons and Fischer in the 1930s. In fact, in many ways Goodhart's summation would fit nicely with Seligman's banking school arguments that the expansion of the money supply, and its subsequent harmful contraction, are the result of borrowing demand, rather than ambitious lending by the banking industry. This latter currency school argument adamantly drove the Chicago

Plan and 100% Money arguments of the 1930s. We will see in the next chapter how the deregulation of the banking industry led to the explosive growth in money supply from the 1970s on. Whether this was a coincidence of wants, that is banks could lend more easily just when borrowers wanted more debt, is beyond the scope of this book. What we deal with here is that the expansion in the money supply, through the expansion in bank (and shadow bank) issued debt, leads to economic volatility as seen in the Great Depression of the 1930s, and the Great financial crisis of 2007/09.

As already mentioned, the creation of a machinery to add reserves to the system as and when required, was fundamentally important to freeing up banking in the United States. Over the course of the 20th century however, the concept that the management of reserves requirements by the central bank impacted upon the expansion of the money supply by the banking industry, through a multiplier effect, has been rejected. In fact, Carpenter & Demiralp (2012)[76] write that central bank reserve requirements have diminished to virtually be non-influential in the determination by banks as to whether they will increase lending or not. That is, the money multiplier is no longer an effective money supply management tool by the central bank. Goodhart (2017: 39) goes further when he says, '[t]he money base multiplier almost never operated in practice; now it is defunct even in theory and in principle.' Instead Goodhart makes clear that the central bank attempts to influence the money supply by setting the interest rate at which banks can borrow reserves, and not the growth rate of the monetary base. In his paper Goodhart discusses the age-old differences between the currency school and the banking school approaches to the money supply. The former he writes about as being the 'controlled' approach to monetary expansion and the latter is the 'flexible' approach where clients are free to borrow from banks as their needs dictate (Goodhart 2017: 36).

The relationship between reserves and deposits however remains an important one, albeit that in today's arrangements reserves are added 'after the fact' as and when needed. In today's world (further discussed in chapter 5) central banks have grown to become more the linchpin in the circuit of money instead of being a supporter on the sidelines. The money supply within a developed economy is still a split circuit system (Huber 2017 (b) - discussed in detail in ch. 6) made up of both government currency and bank deposit liabilities created when granting a loan. Borrowed from Yamaguchi's (2019) Systems Dynamics based approach to money and accounting, Figure 4.2.1 shows this transition (hierarchy) from reserves to loans to deposits.

Figure 4.2.1 - Hierarchy of money stock creation

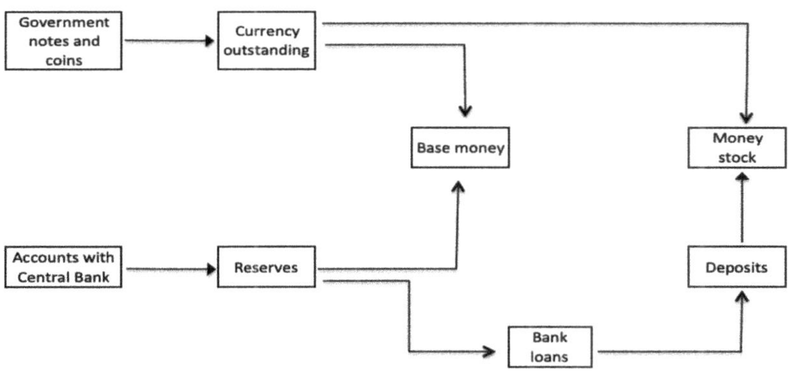

Source: Adapted from Yamaguchi 2019: 130

The money creation process depicted above as 'Money Stock' is designated by the FED as M2 including time deposits. The measure of money used was a differentiating factor between the Chicago Plan and Fisher's 100% Money (see Ch 3) but the purpose of this diagram here is to highlight the two differential flows of media of exchange, and the fact that they do not overlap. Next, we see how these flows are dealt with from an accounting point of view.

4.3 The Bank Balance Sheet

Table 4.3.1 shows how changes in bank reserve balances could determine the size of bank assets and liabilities under the multiplier model. For example, a policy decision by the Fed to add liquidity, in this instance $10,000, would lead through fractional reserve banking, and given a required reserves balance of 10% of deposits, to an expansion of bank deposits from the initial $10,000 to $100,000. That is, 1/.10 x 10,000 = 100,000.

Table 4.3.1 Monetary expansion under fractional reserves banking

		Assets				Liabilities
			Reserves			
		Total	(Required)	(Excess)	Loans and Investments	Deposits
Initial reserves provided		10,000	1,000	9,000	-	10,000
Expansion	Stage 1	10,000	1,900	8,100	9,000	19,000
	Stage 2	10,000	2,710	7,290	17,100	27,100
	Stage 3	10,000	3,439	6,561	24,390	34,390
	Stage 4	10,000	4,095	5,905	30,951	40,951
	Stage 5	10,000	4,686	5,314	36,856	46,856
	Stage 6	10,000	5,217	4,783	42,170	52,170
	Stage 7	10,000	5,695	4,305	46,953	56,953
	Stage 8	10,000	6,126	3,874	51,258	61,258
	Stage 9	10,000	6,513	3,487	55,132	65,132
	Stage 10	10,000	6,862	3,138	58,619	68,619
	-		-	-	-	-
	-		-	-	-	-
	-		-	-	-	-
	Stage 20	10,000	8,906	1,094	79,058	89,058
	-		-	-	-	-
	-		-	-	-	-
	-		-	-	-	-
	Final stage	10,000	10,000	-	90,000	100,000

Source: FED Chicago 1994: 11

4.3.1 How the multiple expansion process works

The above example shows how a system wide bank balance sheet would grow from a start of 10,000 to 100,000, that is a growth of 1000%. This occurs because banks are only mandated to hold a certain fraction of total deposits as reserves. In Table 4.3.1 above it does not matter whether the initial $10,000 deposit sits with any one particular bank. System wide, as the funds are drawn and deposited with other banks, the $10,000 will still exist in total until withdrawn through asset sales by the central bank. This is because banks have individual accounts with the central bank. So that as one bank's reserves are depleted due to the withdrawal of deposits, another bank's account is credited with those same deposits[77] (see Figure 4.3.3 below). However, under the 10% fractional reserve system banks in total need not keep the full $10,000 as a cash asset, only $1,000 is required. The $9,000 in excess reserves can now be invested or lent out by the banking system. Of course they don't lend the physical cash, since if that were the case there would be no expansion of deposits. Banks simply pass book entries denoting the acceptance of an asset and the creation of a liability for an amount of $9,000. Now, $900 only needs to be set aside to fund this creation of new deposits (Stage1 above). From the original cash injection of $10,000, we now have $1,900 funding $19,000 of newly created deposits, leaving $8,100 of cash reserves to continue the funding of newly created deposits (see stages 2 onwards above).[78]

Creditor/debtor relationships are a fundamental building block for any understanding of money and exchange between individuals in a society, both historic and contemporary. In conjunction with the emergence of such a system of interaction has been the development of accounting rules and conventions:

> both formal and informal, both private and public—which define the hierarchy of moneys and which structure the

growth and volume of credit and debt, and the range of its permissible uses. (Bezemer 2016: 1275)

Without such a system to monitor loans issued, payments made, interest accrued and so forth capitalism as we know it today could not have evolved. Yet as Bezemer (2016) points out the relationship of exchange, construed via the debtor/creditor construct and the balance sheet to encompass it has been mostly left out of economic theorising. Where orthodox economists have not considered it important, business practice has and therefore a robust system of accounting has emerged on which we can rely to enhance our understanding of how bank expansion of their balance sheets leads to financial instability.[79]

The CB may well add reserves, but the banks then need to use those reserves to increase their balance sheet. They will only do that if there is customer demand for new borrowings and in fact if the banks see an expansionary phase in the economy. Figure 4.3.1 shows how extra lending flows through to households and businesses at the aggregate system level.

Figure 4.3.1 Aggregate money creation by the banking sector

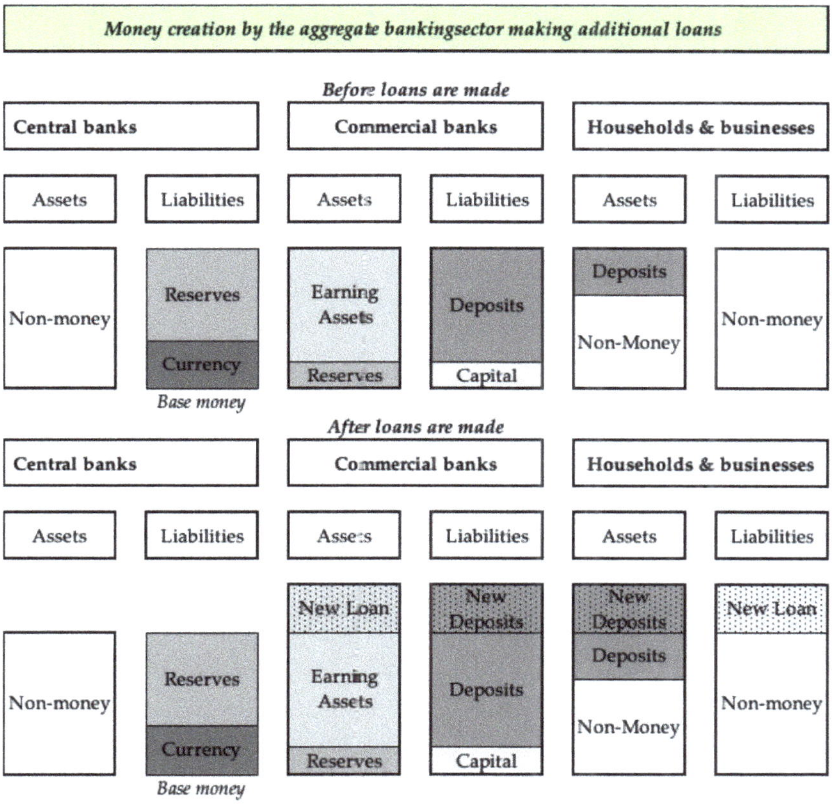

Source: KPMG & Jourdan 2016 and McKLeay et al. 2014. Commercial banks' balance sheet depiction into four primary entries is from Alford 2010.

There are various constraints on bank lending at the individual bank level. These will in the main be dealt with in chapter 5; along with why they seemed to fail. For our purposes here the important constraint is highlighted below where we see the eventual transfer of reserves and deposits from the paying bank to the receiving bank.

Figure 4.3.2 Money creation at the individual bank level

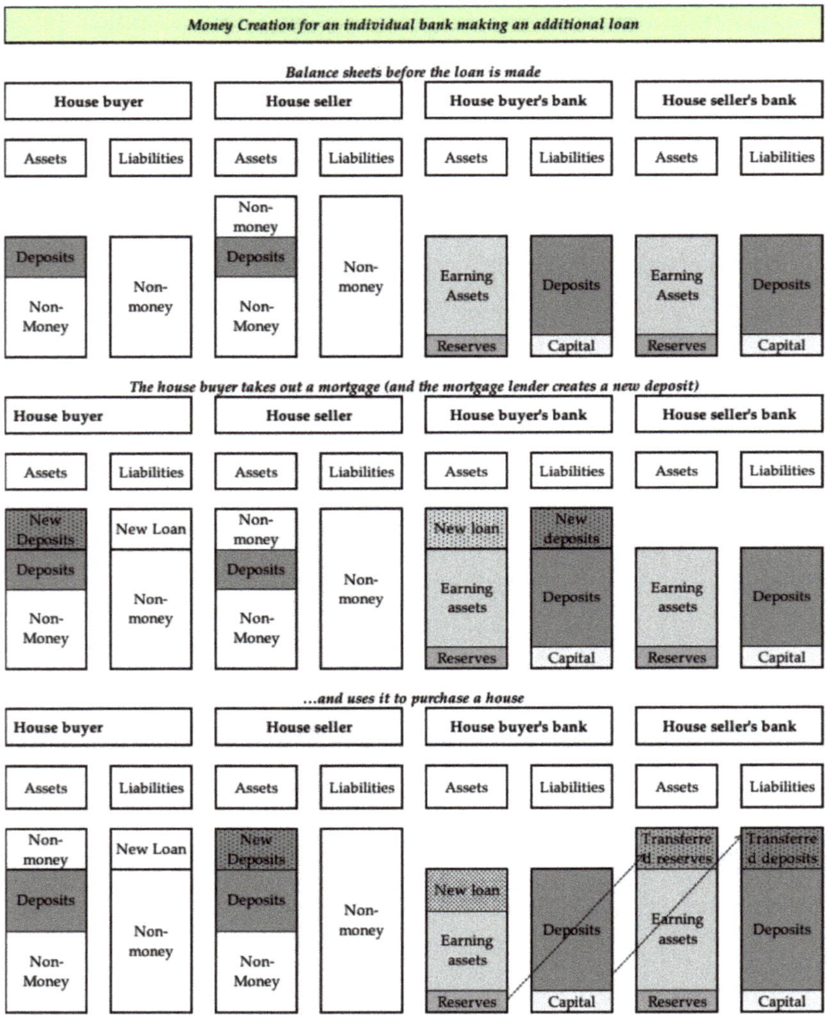

Source: KPMG & Jourdan 2016 and McKLeay et al. 2014. Commercial banks' balance sheet depiction into four primary entries is from Alford 2010.

On the issuance of a new loan by the bank it is to be expected that the newly created deposit[80] would be drawn down by the borrower to pay the seller, since their account would likely be with a different bank. The issuing bank will lose reserves since it needs to drawdown on its account with the central bank to pay the receiving bank's account. On a system wide level that is not likely to be a problem since at the end of the day banks net off payments and receipts and the amount of reserves they need to pay away will only be a fraction of the total transactions.[81] An individual bank that tries to gain market share by aggressively marketing loans, would run the risk of not being able to borrow the required reserves since its payments at the central bank would be much greater than its receipts.[82] In this way the aggregate banking system acts as a leveller in itself. As this essay seeks to portray however, systemic money creation that runs too far ahead of fundamentals runs the risk of engendering a financial bubble (see for example Ravn 2021). The consequences of which runs the risk of a subsequent deflationary bust as seen during the Great Financial Crisis in 2007/09 (Chapter 5).[83]

There is a question that arises because of what we have seen so far regarding bank balance sheets and the financing of industry in general. How is it that banks, through an act of bookkeeping, can generate spending power? Richard Werner looks at this comprehensively. As Werner (2014: 71) says banks are:

> exempted from the Client Money Rules and thus, unlike other firms, do not have to segregate client money. This enables banks to classify their accounts payable liabilities arising from bank loan contracts as a different type of liability called 'customer deposits'.

This allows a $100 deposit to bank ABC by Mrs. Jones to be absorbed into the banks 'deposit liabilities' pool. If banks were obligated to hold client deposits in a segregated client account, similar say to a futures clearing house, then Mrs. Jones' deposit as well as all other client deposits, would not be able to be on-lent, they would need to be fully accounted for (Werner 2014: 76). This, as we will see in chapter 6, is the crux of the Sovereign Money argument. If banks were unable to expand deposits through book entries, and thus generate artificial purchasing power, would this bring Ingham's 'Capitalism' to a grinding halt? As it is argued throughout this thesis, if bank deposits were to be 100% funded, then a major source of financial instability would be aborted since banks would not be able to increase or decrease the money supply. We will drill down into this concept more in a moment, but just to say here that this point lies at the core of the banking crisis of the 1930s and is the spearhead of the arguments poised by Knight, Simons and Fisher. We will soon see what Alford (2010) has to say on this.

4.3.2 Purchasing Power Generated through Bank accounting

What is this peculiar accounting convention that allows banks to generate spending power through bookkeeping? As Werner (2014: 72) says not only is it an arrangement that singularly allocates to banks a monopoly power to generate income from this source, but it is also a 'fact that no law, statute or bank regulation explicitly grants banks the right (usually considered a sovereign prerogative) to create and allocate the money supply'. The next three tables show a loan granted by three types of corporations and how they are reflected on their balance sheets.

Figure 4.3.3 Comparative accounting after the disbursement of a loan

Table 1: Comparative accounting: taking out a loan and disbursing it.

Non Financial Corporation			Non Bank Financial Institution			Bank		
	Assets	Liabilities		Assets	Liabilities		Assets	Liabilities
Loan	+100	0	Loan	+100	0	Loan	+100	+100
Deposit	-100	0	Deposit	-100	0	Deposit		
	0	0		0	0		100	100

Figure 4.3.3 shows the contract signed and finalised with funds allocated. The bank shows the transaction has increased its balance sheet. The NFC and NBFI do not show any change in their balance sheet. This is explained below.

Figure 4.3.4 Step 1 cf loan process - loan approved

Table 2: Disaggregating lending: Step 1 — lender and borrower agree.

Non Financial Corporation				Non Eank Financial Institution				Bank			
	Assets		Liabilities		Assets		Liabilities		Assets		Liabilities
Loan	+100	A/c Payable	+100	Loan	+100	A/c Payable	+100	Loan	+100	A/c Payable	+100
	+100		+100		+100		+100		+100		+100

In Figure 4.3.4 the transaction is frozen in time at the granting of the loan but before disbursement of funds. All corporations have the same balance sheet at this stage showing the asset as the loan and the liability as the account payable but not yet disbursed.

Figure 4.3.5 Step 2 of loan process - funds disbursed

Table 3: Disaggregating lending: Step 2 — loan funds paid out.

Non Financial Corporation				Non Bank Financial Institution				Bank			
	Assets		Liabilities		Assets		Liabilities		Assets		Liabilities
Loan	+100	A/c Payable	0	Loan	+100	A/c Payable	0	Loan	+100	A/c Payable	0
Deposit	-100			Deposit	-100			Deposit		Client Depos	+100
	0		0		0		0		+100		+100

Source: Figures 4.3.3 to 4.3.5 adapted from Werner 2014

Figure 4.3.5 shows the completed transaction. Both the NFC and the NBFI have disbursed the funds to the borrower through debiting their assets. The funds were physically allocated. The bank shows a different approach. There has been no physical disbursement of funds. Instead through an accounting convention the A/c

Payable was morphed into a Client Deposit. The bank balance sheet, unlike the other two, expands on both sides.[85]

Werner's 2014 paper explains further how banks generate purchasing power through the creation of deposits:

> The bank's liability is simply re-named a 'bank deposit'. However, bank deposits are defined by central banks as being part of the official money supply (as measured in such official 'money supply' aggregates as M1, M2, M3 or M4). This confirms that banks create money when they grant a loan: they invent a fictitious customer deposit, which the central bank and all users of our monetary system, consider to be 'money', indistinguishable from 'real' deposits not newly invented by the banks. Thus banks do not just grant credit, they create credit, and simultaneously they create money. (Werner 2014: 74)

If banks create credit (money) when issuing a loan, they also destroy it, and its purchasing power, when the loan is repaid. As Robert Hemphill writes in the foreword to Irving Fisher's book '100% Money' (1936):

> When a bank loan is paid, someone draws on one of these deposits to pay it, and of course so much of that deposits goes out of existence, and a train of successive transactions which would otherwise have been made with that portion of that deposit ceases. (Fisher 1936: XXII)

This point seeks to connect the importance of the bank balance sheet to the actuality of the damage caused to the national economy by the banks having the freedom to imagine a medium of exchange. Especially since as Hemphill continues to say, by allowing "the banks to create ample synthetic money we are prosperous; if not, we starve. We are absolutely without a permanent monetary system" (Fisher 1936: XXII).

4.4 The Alford Cross

The multiplier (fractional reserve) model came into existence as justification for the age-old business premise that the higher the gearing the greater the return. Then of course the other side of that coin is that the higher the gearing the higher the risk. This is the issue at the core of this thesis; the financial and social instability caused by the fact that banks can multiply liabilities, based on an opportunistic view to expand their balance sheet. This is one plank of the Alford Cross to be discussed below and is referred to as the Liquidity Ratio. The other plank of the Alford Cross is the loans to equity ratio. This ratio is geared up by many multiples as well, as the bank seeks to leverage its profitability on an ever relatively shrinking capital base. This is referred to by Alford as the Solvency Ratio. It is the breakdown in the relationships within one or both of these two ratios that leads to economic crisis after economic crisis. The point to belabour here is that money, the media of exchange, regardless of its origination, is sourced as debt. Private institutions generate the media of exchange through the issuance of floating liabilities against fixed assets in the form of book entries. In this section we will also use data provided by the Federal Reserve Board of Governors - FED BG - from the inception of the Federal Reserve System in 1914 to today, to put flesh on the bones of the arguments posed by both Simons, Fisher, Knight in the 1930s and the Sovereign Money promoters of the 2007/09 crisis.

Alford's forensic accounting process is used to provide an interpretation of the FED BG data mentioned above to understand the financial world in which the Chicago Plan for 100% reserves was formulated (though not taken up). We are by now familiar with Alford's bank balance sheet. It is segmented into four components:

on the Assets side we have Earning Assets (EA) and Liquid Assets (LIQ) and on the Liabilities side we have Deposits (DE) and Capital (CAP) (see Figure 4.4.1). To the right is shown Alford's Cross (Alford 2010) highlighting the important balance sheet relationships that he is concerned with.

Figure 4.4.1 Alford's balance sheet approach

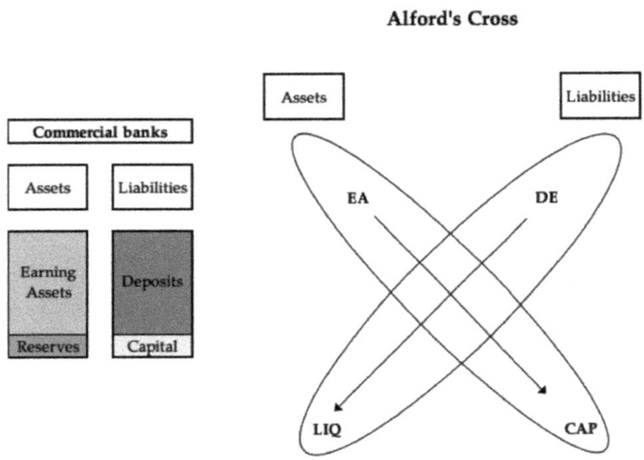

Source: Alford (2010: 3)

Alford saw the liquid and capital assets as the 'potentially fragile points of a bank at which failure can occur and remedial action has to be focussed' (Alford 2010: 2). In the event of a financial shock these are the two points in the individual, as well as systemic banking industry that will need concerted support by the sovereign. As already mentioned, these two balance sheet items are the denominators of the liquidity and solvency ratios respectively, which are further discussed below. The connotation of Alford's analysis as a 'cross' stems from his writings about balance sheet shocks (Alford 2010), which is what we are mainly concerned with here. It is during a crisis impacting upon the financial industry that the relationships between 'risk assets' and 'capital' as one plank of the Alford Cross, along with 'deposits' and 'liquidity' on the other, are sorely tested. The purpose of this type of bank balance sheet analysis is to capture the impacts of any liquidity (reserve assets over deposits) or solvency (capital over risk assets) shocks. This was the case at the time of the Chicago Plan, and it is the case today.

4.4.1 The Solvency and Liquidity Ratios

The Solvency Ratio

According to Alford's schematic bank balance sheet Earning Assets (loans) are supported by Capital. So that profits from assets are after expenses and distributions allocated to capital and conversely losses on earning assets are redeemed from capital. As Alford says (Alford 2010: 4) it is in the interest of the bank to have as high an exposure as possible to $1 of capital to maximise return on capital. With of course a commensurate increase in risk as shown below. This is referred to as the capital or **Solvency Ratio**.

The Liquidity Ratio

As we have seen banks are in the business of making money from loans and investments (plus fees). We have also seen that there is a direct causal correlation between earning assets and deposits. That is, the bank 'creates' its deposit to pay for its investment. Deposits are liquid liabilities and must be paid for, on withdrawal or when the depositor pays someone who has an account with another bank, by the bank's reserves of liquid assets. Alford refers to this relationship as the **Liquidity Ratio**.

Basel III

In contemporary times how much money a bank keeps as liquid assets to meet its liquid liabilities is at the prerogative of the bank, albeit maintaining minimum leverage and liquidity coverage ratios as proposed by the Basel III agreement.

Figure 4.4.2 Solvency shock leading to a liquidity shock - The Alford Cross

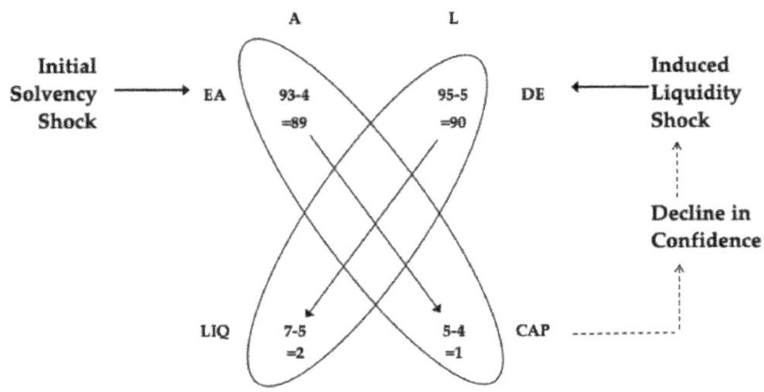

Source: Alford (2010: 9)

Figure 4.4.2 shows how a loss in Earning Assets from 93 units to 89 units (-4.3%) leads to a much greater impact on Capital of 5 units down to 1 unit (-80% due to the gearing of 18.6). This leads to a decline in confidence which then spills over into a withdrawal of liquidity from the bank. Deposits fall from 95 units down to 90 units (-5.3%), which creates a drop in Liquidity from 7 units to 2 units (-71% due to a liquidity gearing ratio of 13.6).

Although with a different purpose in mind, Goodhart sets out a similar schematic for the bank balance sheet (Table 4.4.1). Whereas Alford is seeking to explain the impact of shocks to the bank balance sheet, and the subsequent repairs that are required by the central bank, Goodhart is exploring the relationship between loan assets and deposit liabilities, and what needs to 'shift' for the balance sheet to be equal on both sides.

Table 4.4.1 Goodhart's Balance Sheet

Assets	Liabilities
Cash Reserves (R)	Deposits (D)
Loans (L)	Capital (K)

$$R + L = D + K$$

Source: Goodhart (1989: 228)

He writes:

> If the volume of deposits is determined by the demand function for money, at the policy determined level of market interest rates, what forces ensure that $R + L = D + K$ at every single moment? (Goodhart 1989: 228)

Goodhart makes the point that since the demand for credit is not the same as the demand for money, and since the balance sheet must always balance, then either loans or deposits are subservient to the other (given a fixed capital and a fixed reserves ratio). He finds that the side that generally gives way is the deposits since loan amounts tend to be fixed whereas the acceptance of money balances is more flexible. In other words, it is assumed that households and businesses make deliberate decisions to borrow whereas they are happy to accept money balances at any time. The 'total deposits' component of the balance sheet is therefore composed of temporary demand for money balances and a more fixed demand for credit. As he says:

> Put another way, at any point of time, the demand for credit at given interest rates determines the stock of money - in theory the reverse might have been true, with the demand for money at given interest rates determining the volume

> of bank credit. In markets as they actually exist, it is the former, not the latter, that happens to be more generally true (Goodhart 1989: 229).

Deposits are a factor of loans, and deposits are bank liabilities and loans are customer liabilities. Since deposits are treated as money, and since they make up around 95% of total money supply, then for Goodhart's balance sheet to balance, the money supply within a modern economy is in the main constituted from debt.

Irving Fisher was already greatly concerned with the fact that the money supply is in the main constituted from debt, well before Goodhart wrote those words. He saw the relationship as being a dysfunctional one in that commercial banks seemed to produce more of it when it wasn't needed and reduce its supply just when it was needed the most:

> That was the situation for several years, everybody waiting for somebody else to go into debt to the banks in order to supply the public with the circulating medium which all needed. Finally the government stepped in and itself went deeply into debt with the banks (Fisher 1936: 105).

As Fisher saw it this would continue to be a problem under the then 10% fractional reserve system. And it would continue to be so whilst the circulating medium was a biproduct of private debt. Banks however are in business to make money and through increased leverage of liquidity and capital reserves, comes a greater potential for greater profits. But as the economic crises of the 1930s and the 2000s demonstrate, the end result can also be catastrophic economic malaise. Alford's depiction of a bank balance sheet serves to highlight how through over extension and lack of prudential behaviour; the solvency and liquidity ratios can become over geared as banks lead an economy into speculative upswings. The potential subsequent downswing leads to a solvency induced lack of confidence with potential to feed into a liquidity shock. This was the argument put by Simons, Knight, Fisher and many more academics and economists in the 1930s. Chapter 5 will show that what was true in the 1930s is also true today.

4.4.2 The Alford Cross and the Great Depression Banking Crisis.

FED BG Data

The Board of Governors of the Federal Reserve System in the U.S.A., FED BG, sought to make available in one publication a set of comprehensive statistics on the evolution and performance of banks in the U.S. It did this by issuing two volumes - Banking and Monetary Statistics 1914-1941 and Banking and Monetary Statistics 1941-1970. The data appears as a .pdf file available through the digitised for Frazer library at the federal Reserve Bank of StLouis (http:/fraser.stlouisfed.org/). The balance sheet data used here for all Member Banks of the Federal Reserve System was drawn from table 18 on pages 65 to 75. It should be noted that over the period in question although member banks only comprised "30 to 45 per cent of all commercial banks" in the 1920s it still covered "70 per cent and in recent years about 85 per cent of total deposits of all commercial banks" (Banking and Monetary Statistics 1914-1941: 5). Figure 4.4.4 shows all the categories reported on by the FED BG data. The greyed-out boxes are the data sets used here to compile Alford's four main balance sheet categories.

Table 4.4.2 Balance sheet categories used in the Alford Cross

Balance Sheet Category	Sub-categories				
Total Earning Assets	Total Loans	Total Investments	Investments U.S. Government obligations	Investments Other securities	
Total Liquid Assets	Reserves with Federal Reserve Banks	Cash in vault	Balances with domestic banks	Balances with foreign banks	Cash items in process of collection
Total Deposits	Interbank	U.S. Government	Postal savings	Other demand deposits	Other time deposits
Total Capital	Common stock	Preferred stock	Surplus	Undivided profits	Reserves for Contingencies

Source: FED BG Banking and Monetary Statistics 1914-1941

Alford depicts these four categories as being sufficient to explain 95% of the major events impacting upon banks' balance sheets (Alford 2010: 5). They are: 1) Total Earning Assets; 2) Total Liquid Assets; 3) Total Deposits; 4) Total Capital. I have taken a broad approach to the data in that a) I am using annual closing data and b) I use the Dec 1929 data point as the peak and the Dec 1933 data point as the bottom of this deflationary cycle. This analysis does not depend on the actual traded points in size and time but rather is looking at the meta trends in play. In Table 4.4.3 the data drawn from FED BG is compared to the statistics used by Fisher in his 1936 book 100% Money (pages 5-7).

Table 4.4.3 Comparing BG (Fed) data with Fisher 1936 data

USD Millions

	Total Loans	Other demand deposits	Total Capital	Total Liquid Assets	BG (FED) Money Supply	Fisher (1936: 6) Money Supply	Velocity	BG (FED) Total Circulation	Fisher (1936: 6) Total Circulation
Dec-29	26,150	20,543	6,710	5,828	27,371	27,000	30.0	821,130	810,000
Dec-33	12,833	13,807	4,962	4,281	18,088	20,000	20.0	361,760	400,000
Difference	(13,317)	(6,736)	(1,748)	(2,547)	(9,283)	(7,000)	(10.0)	(459,370)	(410,000)
as %	-50.9%	-32.8%	-26.1%	-37.3%	-33.9%	-25.9%	-33.3%	-55.9%	-50.6%

Source: BG (Fed) Banking and Monetary Statistics 1914-1941; Fisher Money Supply and Velocity estimates are from Fisher 1936: 5-7.

Of note is that Fisher did not include 'time Deposits' in his demand deposits since as already described in section 3.3.3 above Fisher did not believe that time deposits constituted the circulating medium. Therefore, for comparison purposes the FED BG data used here also excludes time deposits. As Fisher wrote the close relationship between bank risk assets (loans) and the deposits they create 'constitute the great defects in our present banking system' (Fisher 1936: 47). The 50% shrinkage in bank loans translated into a nearly 33% collapse in on demand deposits. Figure 4.4.5 adds demand deposits to total liquid assets to arrive at the money supply, as Fisher would have done. The 30% drop in the money supply meant, as Fisher (1936: 6) wrote:

> That destruction of 8 billion dollars of what the public counted on as their money was the chief sinister fact in the depression from which followed the two chief tragedies, unemployment and bankruptcies.

Using the data in Table 4.4.3 I construct the Alford Cross as seen below in Figure 4.4.3. Note that the amounts are shown in billions rather than millions.

Figure 4.4.3 Solvency shock that led to liquidity shock in the early 1930s

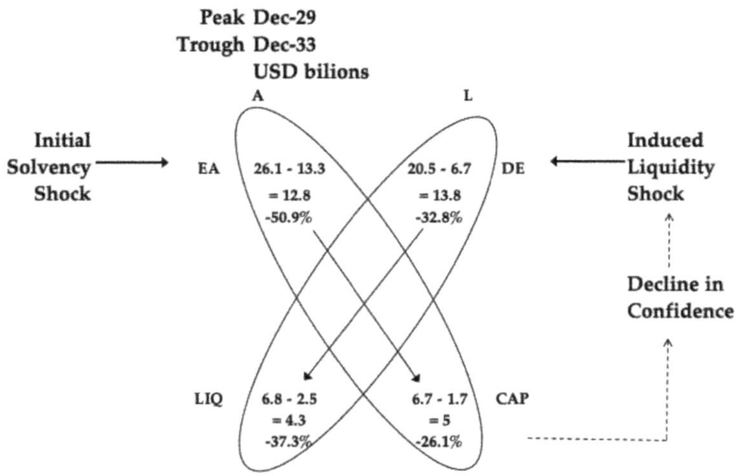

Source: Data from FED BG Banking and Monetary Statistics 1914-1941

As Figure 4.4.3 shows between Dec 1929 and Dec 1933 there was a reduction in bank earning assets (EA) of 13.3 billion dollars and a reduction in bank deposits of 6.7 billion dollars. Loan repayments reduce deposit liabilities as well as earning assets and so do not impact bank capital. According to Alford's methodology a loss write off by the bank will however impact upon bank equity, so that out of the 13.3 billion reduction in EA 11.6 billion would be loan repayments and 1.7 billion would be losses written off, since CAP has fallen from 6.7 to 5 billion dollars. Gearing within the balance sheet meant that the loss of 6.1% (1.7/26.1) in EA became a loss of 26.1% in bank equity (CAP). The dangers posed by the nearly 4 X gearing in the Solvency Ratio are immediately obvious. The other side of the 50% reduction in EA was a 32.8% reduction in bank deposits (DE) or 'check book money' (Fisher 1936). Part of the total reduction in DE of 6.7 billion dollars would have been loan repayments since they reduce both EA and DE, and the other part, 2.5 billion, would have been money withdrawals because of the run on banks. As the bank liquidity (LIQ) numbers show there was a 2.5 billion reduction in actual 'pocketbook money (Fisher 1936) representing 37.3% reduction of total bank liquidity. In 100%Money (1936) Fisher talks about a loss in 'check book money' of 8 billion dollars between 1929 and 1936, roughly matching these numbers drawn from FED BG. This was singularly the major contribution to what would become the Great Depression of the 1930s (see section 3.2 above), and according to the monetary reformists of the times, was a crucial justification for approaches such as the Chicago Plan or 100% money. As Fisher wrote:

> [t]he public was forced to sacrifice 8 billion dollars out of 23 billions of the main circulating medium which would not have been sacrificed had the 100% system been in use (fisher 1936: 7).

It was not only the reduction in the quantity of money that led to the devastating economic contraction of the 1930s, but also the rate of its annual turnover. Fisher (1936: 6) estimates the money velocity dropped from 30x in 1929 to 20x in 1933. The total circulation of the media of exchange therefore halved from around 800 billion in 1929 to 400 billion in 1933 (see Table 4.4.3 above) leading to the economic contraction described in Section 3.2 above.

4.4.3 Dismantling of the Alford Cross

When the highly geared earning assets and deposits components of the balance sheet have a sharp drop, the impacts on the cash and capital balance sheet items are magnified, and sometimes to the demise of an individual institution if not the aggregate system itself. This impact can be seen in Figure 4.4.3 above. The relationship between economic activity and the money stock can be described by the chicken and egg metaphoric scenario. Regardless, Alford clearly shows the impact of a decrease in bank earning assets, which would transcribe into decreased economic activity. As this feeds into a solvency shock, there is the potential for a liquidity shock to arise since depositors will become concerned at the banks' decreasing capital condition and will begin withdrawing their money. This then leads to further asset sales by the banks as they seek to raise more liquidity and so on onto a crash scenario.[86] Figure 4.4.4 shows how this entire process is potentially avoided through the Chicago Plan 100% reserves proposal.

Figure 4.4.4 Avoidance of a Solvency shock leading to a liquidity shock

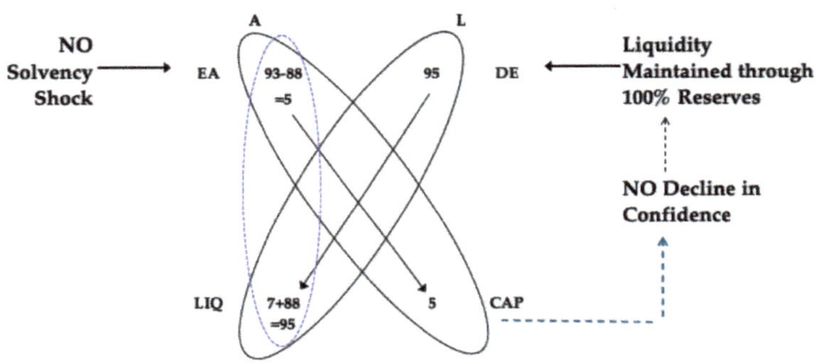

Source: Adapted from Alford 2010: 9

In Figure 4.4.4 there are initially 95 units of customer deposits (DE) supported by 7 units of liquidity (LIQ). The Chicago Plan and Fisher's 100% Money plan both wanted to totally fund the deposits (there was disagreement as to the extent of the deposits base to be funded as described in chapter 3) so that a total of 88 units had to be injected in bank LIQ accounts. To achieve this some government entity would purchase 88 units of earning assets (EA) from the banks crediting the bank's cash account by the same amount, leaving bank liquidity at 95 units, matching deposits of 95 units. Now every $1 of cheque deposits has $1 of real money supporting it. The net result would be that the additional injection of cash by the Government would not impact on the existing level of the medium of exchange. The extra cash is simply the mirror of the existing cheque deposits. This would then enable the dismantling of the Alford Cross. The DE/LIQ plank could be safely removed from the EA/CAP plank leaving two distinct entities as shown in Figure 4.4.5.

Figure 4.4.5 The Alford Cross Dismantled

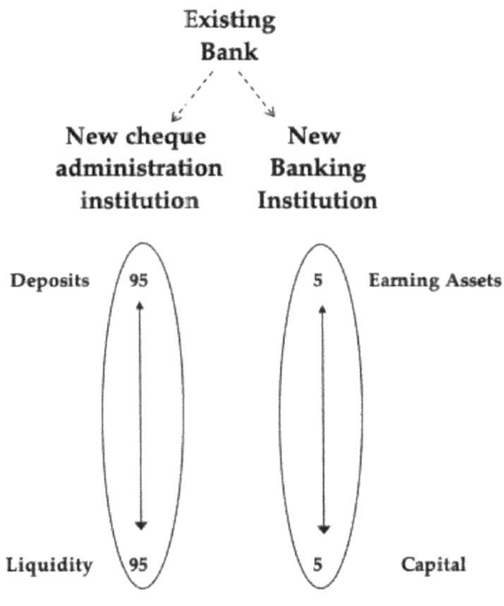

Source: Adapted from Alford 2010

The Chicago Plan would have been fully enacted had this approach been accepted by the Roosevelt administration in the 1930s. This example has ignored Angell's (1935) criticism as to which assets would be bought by the government and it was readily admitted by the Chicago Plan adherents that the practicalities of its implementation remained to be resolved (see Chapter 3). These apparently intractable issues appear to be resolved within the Sovereign Money debate as will be seen below. What the above schematics clearly show though is the attractiveness of a solution where there is no contagion between the banking industry's quest for profits through risk taking, and a caretaker role for the broader community's savings.

4.5 Conclusion

This chapter began by placing quite a lot of importance on an assessment of the determination of the money supply. The impetus for this is the fact that the medium of exchange enters the system as bank liabilities and is created by banks passing balance sheet entries. This function was well described by Vanderlip in 1908 and was written about by Frederick Soddy, Frank Knight, Henry Simons, Irving Fisher and many other academics of the early 1900s. Yet it has been sidelined through the remainder of the twentieth century. By using Alford's simplified methods for assessing the bank balance sheet, we can understand the risks of the creation of deposits through loans and the importance of the liquidity and solvency ratios. The possibility of contagion from solvency crisis to liquidity crisis is always extant due to the current practices of banking. This occurred in the 1930s and led to hoarding of cash, which led to thousands of bank closures and great pain and suffering in what was to be called the Great Depression. As we will soon see, the same result was avoided in the 2007/09 crisis because the FED acted quickly and in a very large measure to add liquidity to the system.

Alford's balance sheet technique clearly demonstrates the central argument of the Chicago Plan. That is, that it was necessary to separate the relationship and contagion between the solvency and liquidity ratios. They had to be isolated so that there would be no linkage between Earning Assets and Liquidity. If a bank made investments, those investments could only be funded by actual dollar for dollar cash and therefore there would be no spillover from a solvency shock to a liquidity shock. Depositors would be protected and the banks holding the deposits would not be insolvent and lose customer wealth leading to depression. The 100% reserve banking platform proposed by the Chicago Plan relates to the liquidity of bank liabilities. The balance sheet approach seeks to highlight the connection between solvency and liquidity and how the former can spill over onto the latter to cause bank runs and economic panic. It is the nature of the beast and as we have already seen it is what Knight, Simons and Fisher were yelling about. Now we move to another major economic crisis, the Great financial crisis of 2007/09. Yet another financial crisis caused essentially by the same contradictory banking constructs as existed in the Great depression of the 1930s.

Chapter 5

'Can it Happen Again?' - from the Great Depression to the Great Recession

5.1 Introduction

The Great Financial Crisis (GFC) was at its roots the same as the Great Depression in that the final arbiter in a split circuit money system was a scurry into the sanctuary of cash or primary, that is Federal Reserve, money. They did however differ in two important ways. The first major difference lies in the central bank's reactions to the crisis. It has already been discussed in chapter 3 that the great failure of the 1930s was that of the Federal Reserve to add liquidity. This was certainly not the case in the 2000s where the Federal Reserve, under Ben Bernanke, flooded the system with liquidity.[87] The second major difference between the two crises is that the financial system today is vastly different to what it was in the 1930s. This was acknowledged by the official inquiry into the GFC when it stated in its report that 'We had a 21st-century financial system with 20th-century safeguards.' (FCIC 2010: xx). In this chapter we set the scene for and investigate the impacts of what has come to be known as the Great Financial Crisis (GFC) of 2007/09. Akin to the Great Depression in scope and potential economic fallout, the GFC is marked for the massive central bank interventions that occurred in a bid to rescue not only banks that were 'too big to fail' (TBTF), but the global financial system as a whole.

The liquidity crises of the 1930s and the 2000s prompted the Chicago Plan and 100% Money debates of the 1930s, and the Sovereign Money Creation debates post GFC and 2009. Connecting both crises was the fact that they were born and bred in an ether of debt. Section 5.2 deals with this growth in debt, which in essence is a factor of the evolution of finance as the preponderous input into our social lives. This normative problem eludes solution because at the core of the issuance of the medium of exchange there remains a bank liability, or debt. Section 5.2 questions the marked dichotomy that is observable in the evolution of finance over two distinct periods, the Golden Era of Capitalism from the 1930s to the end of the 1970s, and the Neoliberal Era from the late 1970s to today. We will see that under the tight regulatory controls that evolved during the Great Depression, that the debt to GDP ratio stabilised around 1.5:1. This changed dramatically from the commencement of the Neoliberal Era in the late 1970s that saw debt to GDP ratios reach much higher at around 4:1. What the economic data encompassing this latter period shows is obvious: there has been an overemphasis on debt creation far beyond the requirements of production.[88] Alongside this growth in debt there has been a concomitant requirement for liquidity, which under periods of financial stress, and due to the extreme gearing of assumptions about future value over the realities of present value, has led to massive central bank liquidity injections to preserve the viability of the banking system.

The term 'Too Big to Fail' was first coined by Republican House Representative Stewart McKinney in 1984 in reference to the bailout of Continental Illinois National Bank (CINB). We deal with this in section 5.3 in some detail due to its importance as a harbinger of what was to come. The CINB banking crisis highlights and connects with the worst fears of Simons, Knight and Fisher. Banks, according to their thinking, could not be entrusted to both issue the medium of exchange and perform traditional banking roles as the intermediaries between borrowers and savers. There was a definite role for the state in doing the former, whilst banks occupied themselves with the latter. Through the Congressional Inquiry (St Germain 1984) held by the Committee on Banking and Finance towards the end of 1984, into the collapse and subsequent bailout of Continental Illinois National Bank, we get a look 'inside the kimono' at the mismanagement by CINB senior executives and the failures of the necessary regulatory oversight which led to what was to be the largest banking collapse from the Great Depression to the Great Financial Crisis.

In partnership with the removal of regulatory restrictions finance became increasingly ingenious in developing new ways to extract profits from the future income streams of businesses and households. Alongside all of this sprang financial institutions that were able to operate even further away from regulatory oversight. In section 5.4 we can only touch on this, but it must be noted that these 'shadow banks' play an important part in the development of increasingly complex and derivative financial products to further squeeze present value from future income streams. We demonstrate that conjoining these two eras is the fundamental need for liquidity by the finance industry, and through them society at large. It seems that the role of the central bank is to placate the finance industry by supplying this liquidity when required. The FCIC (2010) report resonates with the earlier St Germain (1984) Inquiry in that they both criticised the inability of the authorities and regulators to spot and forewarn about the increasing bank balance sheet fragilities. Section 5.5 concludes.

5.2 Bridging the Gap with Debt

Using the amply available data over the period bridging these two economic crises, and subsequent inquiries for monetary reform, it is possible to empirically demonstrate the impact that banks have on the broader economy through their control of the money supply. The balance sheet data available in the U.S. for all domestically chartered commercial banks allows us to see the evolution of the liquidity and solvency ratios described by Alford in the previous chapter. As we will soon see in section 5.4, the growth in bank balance sheets also fuelled expansions in speculative markets and the over-gearing of liquidity again, proved the undoing of overzealous lending by banks. According to Alford's Cross (see 4.3 above) the internal relationships within the bank balance sheet, both at the single bank level and the system level, provide valuable insights into the health condition of the banking system. Specifically, the Liquidity and Solvency ratios provide warning signs of overstretched conditions that may lead to a collapse of the financial system were it not for central bank lender of last resort facilities (see Alford 2010: 4). This over-gearing stems from either the asset side or the liabilities side of the balance sheet. In some instances, the series of charts below shows the gyrations of these balance sheet relationships through the lens of a Base 1000 Index to homogenise the relative growth or decline of bank lending activities against related moves in measures of economic growth (GDP) and speculative indices (DJIA). The charts demonstrate the relative cumulative growth of each time series. Bank balance sheet data is drawn from the Board of Governors of the Federal Reserve[90] from 1914 to the present day.

5.2.1 The Golden Years of Capitalism and the Neoliberal Era

The eighty years or so separating the Great Depression and the GFC can broadly be defined as two economic periods: the Golden Age of Capitalism, post WWII to late the 1970s and the Neoliberal Era of Globalisation from the late 1970s to the present time (Juego & Schmidt 2009, Vercelli 2017/2019, Chick 2013, Johnson & Kwak 2010). Vercelli (2017: 43) clearly defines in depth the evolution of

Neoliberalism in the 1970s and its difference in meaning to the term as applied in the early twentieth century. Our concern here though is to delineate between the era when banking was still under tight control and the era when banking had almost complete freedom to expand their balance sheets. This follows from Henry Simons, Frank Knight and Irving Fisher, amongst many other scholars of the 1930s, who believed that the state had a definite and important part to play in managing the financial markets. As we will see this delineation of powers is also the intent of the Sovereign Money Creation debate which, as with the 100% reserves debate of the 1930s, seeks to curb the power of the banks to conflate their two functions as caretakers of society's savings, and as intermediaries between savers and investors.

Vercelli (2017/2019) and Juego & Schmidt (2009) amongst many others date the commencement of the neoliberal globalisation of the world economy from the late 1970s. For our purposes we take December 1979 as the demarcation point based on the election of Margaret Thatcher in the UK And Ronald Reagan in the U.S. (Vercelli 2017). There are of course many other points that could have been taken but the overall outcome would have been roughly similar. That outcome is, to demonstrate through a series of charts, that the growth in bank balance sheets has not been matched by a proportional growth in income as measured by Nominal GDP. Figure 5.2.1 shows the total data set from 1914 to 2021. This chart portrays at the outset, the different rates of growth of debt and productivity within the two economic eras. As the chart (and Table 5.2.1 below) shows Debt[91] to GDP rose from 39.4% in December 1933 to 160.9% in December 1979 with an average Debt/GDP ratio of 121.4% (index to the right-hand scale). By comparison Debt to GDP rose from 160.9% in December 1979 to 372.1% in June 2021 with an average Debt/GDP ratio of 283.1% for the period. These measurements infer that the growth in synthetic liquidity created through debt has been going elsewhere, but certainly not into productivity.

Figure 5.2.1 Two very different economic eras

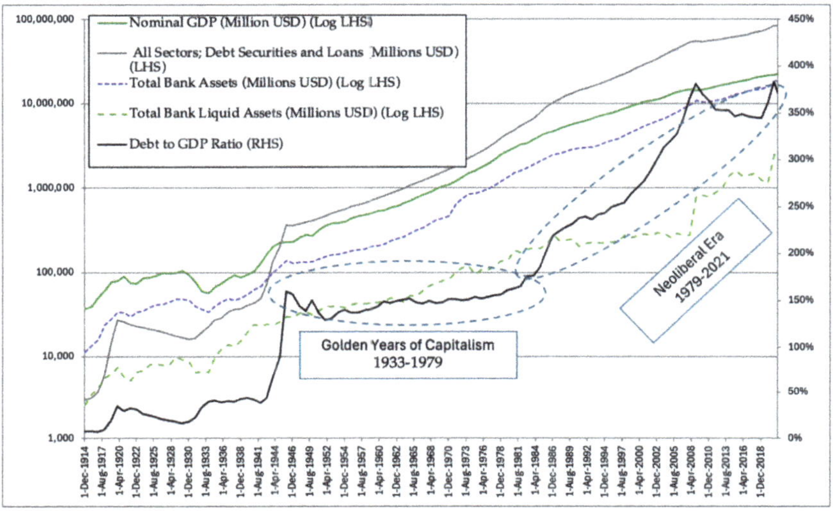

Source: Bank balance sheet: FED BG H.8 Assets and Liabilities of Domestically Chartered Commercial Banks in the United States; Debt: https://fred.stlouisfed.org/series/TCMDO; GDP: https://fred.stlouisfed.org/series/GDP; Debt to GDP: calculations by author.

The chart above shows the steady horizontal move in Debt to GDP that lasted from the end of WWII to roughly 1979. Throughout this period debt appeared to keep pace with GDP growth. In fact, every extra $1.50 of debt procured provided around $1 of GDP. This began to change markedly after the commencement of neoliberal reforms in the 1970s and appears to gain pace as we progress through the end of the twentieth century and commencement of the twenty-first. This is apparent in the Debt to GDP ratio benchmarked to the right-hand scale. The liquidity injected into the economy by banks and the FED does not appear to have a material impact on nominal GDP. In fact, the divergence between the two increases rapidly so that today around $4 of debt is required to generate $1 of GDP. One may ask the question where has the liquidity gone? One avenue of growth matching and in fact surpassing (due to leverage) liquidity growth is that of the Dow Jones Industrial average. Another avenue not shown here would be property. Figures 5.2.2 and 5.2.3 below compare the rates of growth of the speculative share market to GDP over the two periods. As we can see the share market indicator has apparently benefitted handsomely from bank balance sheet expansion over the last 40 years plus. Debt has risen substantially as have asset markets, so where does that leave asset markets over production? Clearly a larger proportion of debt funding is now being allocated to speculative financial assets, including property. This increased creation of debt was referred to by Schumpeter, citing Fisher, as excess debt and as Fisher along with Simons and Knight have also already described, excess debt is the harbinger of financial crisis.[92]

Figure 5.2.2 The Golden Years of Capitalism - Relative Growth

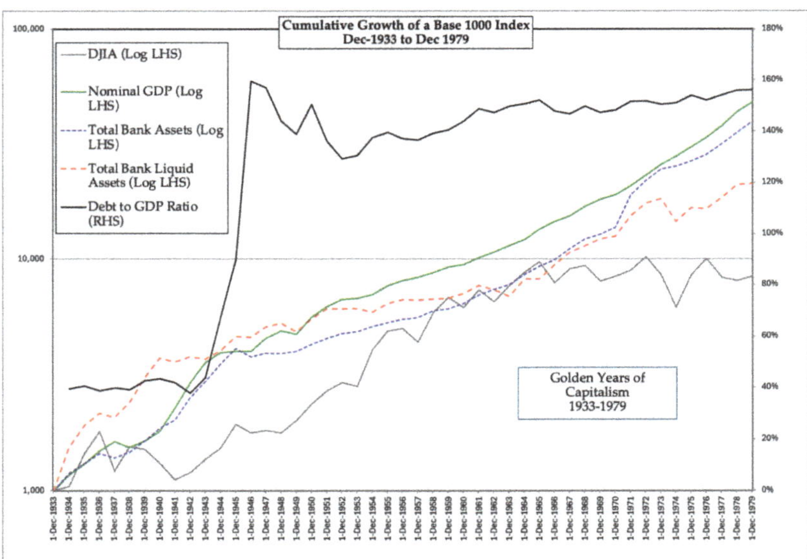

Source: Bank balance sheet: FED BG H.8 Assets and Liabilities of Domestically Chartered Commercial Banks in the United States; Debt: https://fred.stlouisfed.org/

series/TCMDO; GDP: https://fred.stlouisfed.org/series/GDP; Debt to GDP: calculations by author; DJIA: Samuel H. Williamson, 'Daily Closing Value of the Dow Jones Average, 1885 to Present,' MeasuringWorth, 2021; Base 1000 index calculations by author.

Figure 5.2.3 The Neoliberal Era - Relative Growth

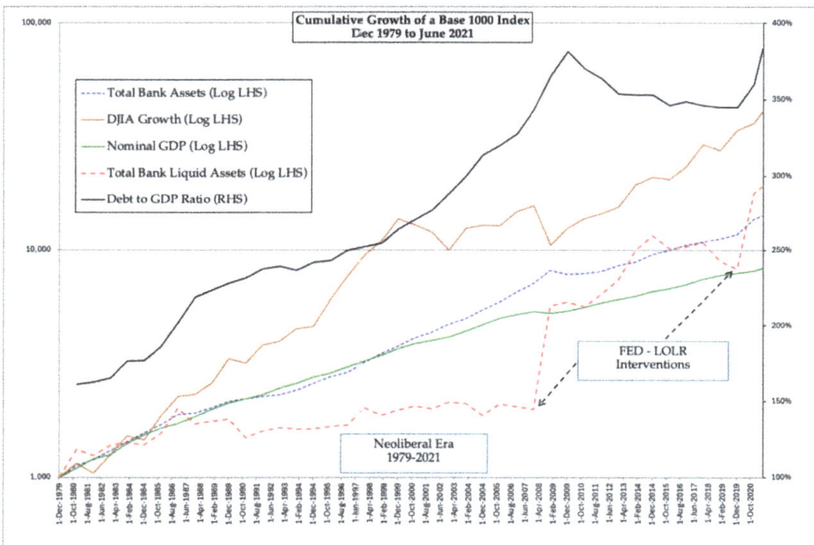

Source: Bank balance sheet: FED BG H.8 Assets and Liabilities of Domestically Chartered Commercial Banks in the United States; Debt: https://fred.stlouisfed.org/series/TCMDO; GDP: https://fred.stlouisfed.org/series/GDP; Debt to GDP: calculations by author; DJIA: Samuel H. Williamson, 'Daily Closing Value of the Dow Jones Average, 1885 to Present,' MeasuringWorth, 2021; Base 1000 index calculations by author

In Figures 5.2.2 and 5.2.3, instead of actual numbers we have calculated a growth index with a Base of 1000 commencing December 1933 and December 1979 respectively. This allows for a meaningful comparison of the cumulative growth between differing asset classes and bank balance sheet values. This author believes that capitalism, and by inference finance, has a directional momentum and that is reflected in the above charts.[93] Some clues to this are provided by Smithin (2013, 2016) when he discusses the need for the ever growth of the money supply. How else is the next entrepreneur to realise their profits if new money is not created by the present one borrowing more? That is not to say that this rise is without the occasional setbacks. Reversals in fortune however are becoming less in time if not in amplitude, as the central banks, the keepers and protectors of capitalism, are becoming more adapt at re-liquifying the markets when they need it (as shown in Figure 5.3.1 below).

Of note in the above two charts is the replacement of Nominal GDP in the first epoch by the speculative share price index, the DJIA, in the second as the growth leader. As Table 5.2.1 below shows, GDP grew from 1933 to 1979 by a total of 4,662%. The total growth of the DJIA was 740% over the same period. The same returns for the Neoliberal Era are almost diametrically opposed. GDP grew by 734% whilst the speculative DJIA grew 4,014%. The freeing up of the banks over the neoliberal era has led to the vast amounts of liquidity generated by both the banking system and through FED interventions into the speculative share market (amongst other asset bubbles such as property that are not shown here) rather than to productive purposes.

Table 5.2.1 Changes in bank balance sheet and economic indicators over the two economic eras

	Total Earning Assets - Banks $ Millions	Total Capital - Banks ($ Millions)	Solvency Ratio	Total Deposits - Banks ($Millions)	Total Liquid Assets - Banks ($ Millions)	Liquidity Ratio	Dow Jones Industrial Average	Nominal GDP ($ Millions)	All Sectors; Debt Securities and Loans ($ Millions)	Debt to GDP Ratio	U.S. Consumer Price Index Average 1982-1984 = 100	Value of $1 in 1914 - CPI based	Velocity (GDP/Money supply)
Dec-1933	25,219	4,962	19.68%	27,167	6,471	23.82%	100	57,200	22,537	39.4%	13.2	0.66	1.70
Dec-1979	1,066,690	105,261	9.87%	1,032,504	137,628	13.33%	839	2,723,883	4,382,456	160.9%	76.7	0.10	2.33
Dec-2021	14,634,739	1,968,201	13.45%	15,932,492	2,674,858	16.79%	34,503	22,722,581	84,564,427	372.2%	271.0	0.03	1.22

	Growth/ (-) Decline Total Earning Assets (Banks)	Growth/ (-) Decline Total Capital (Banks)	Growth/ (-) Decline Solvency Ratio	Growth/ (-) Decline Total Deposits (Banks)	Growth/ (-) Decline Total Liquid Assets (Banks)	Growth/ (-) Decline Liquidity Ratio	Growth/ (-) Decline Dow Jones Industrial Average	Growth/ (-) Decline Nominal GDP	All Sectors; Debt Securities and Loans	Debt to GDP Ratio	Growth/ (-) Decline U.S. Consumer Price Index Average 1982-1984 = 100	Growth/ (-) Decline Value of $1 in 1933 to 2021 - CPI based	Velocity (GDP/Money supply)
Dec 1933 - Dec 1979	4130%	2021%	-50%	3701%	2027%	-44%	740%	4662%	19346%	308%	481%	-85%	37%
Dec 1979 - Dec 2021	1272%	1770%	36%	1443%	1844%	26%	4014%	734%	1830%	131%	253%	-73%	-48%

Source: Bank balance sheet: FED BG H.8 Assets and Liabilities of Domestically Chartered Commercial Banks in the United States; Debt: https://fred.stlouisfed.org/series/TCMDO; GDP: https://fred.stlouisfed.org/series/GDP; CPI: https://fred.stlouisfed.org/series/CPIAUCSL; M2: https://fred.stlouisfed.org/series/M2NS; DJIA: Samuel H. Williamson, 'Daily Closing Value of the Dow Jones Average, 1885 to Present,' MeasuringWorth, 2021;

5.2.2 The Solvency and Liquidity Ratios Over the Two Eras

Liquid assets as a percentage of total bank assets remained fairly stable until the 1970s. There was a marked divergence however between those two measures from the mid 1980s until the present day. From the liberalisation of banking in the early 1980s to the advent of the GFC in 2007/09 the liquidity ratio for banks in the U.S. fell by more than 50% (Figure 5.2.4). This occurred regardless of the drive by banks to seek fee income through origination and distribution rather than traditional lending (Johnson & Kwak 2010: 76). In fact, the securitisation process removed the requirements of banks to assure themselves of the capacity to repay by end users. That risk was passed on to the end purchaser of the security. The systemic risk that began to creep into the financial regime consequently was undetected by all. Kohn (2010: 4) admitted as much when he wrote: 'Serious deficiencies with these securitizations, the associated derivative instruments, and the structures that evolved to hold securitized debt were at the heart of the financial crisis.' But as we will now see, before arriving at the GFC of 2007/09 there was a collapse of a major bank in 1984 that could have served as a warning shot across the bows for the authorities when considering further deregulation of the banking industry. It was not heeded.

Figure 5.2.4 The Solvency and Liquidity ratios over the two economic eras

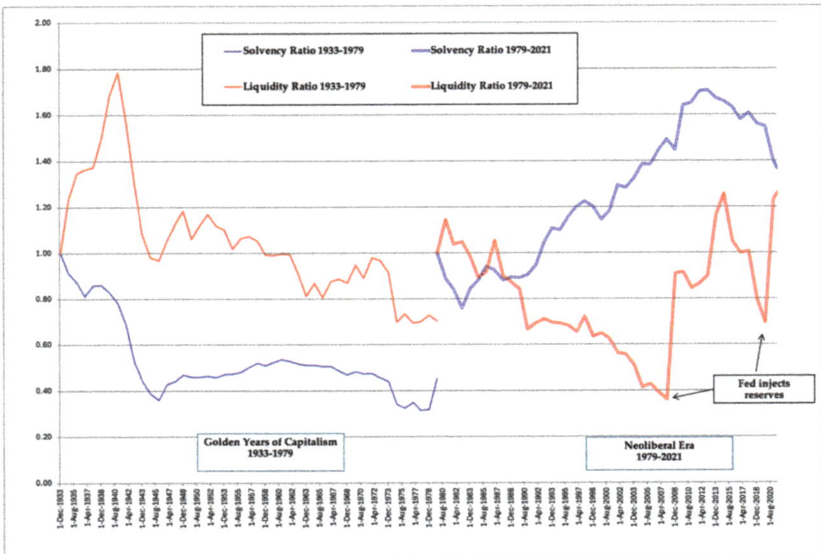

Source: Bank balance sheet: FED BG H.8 Assets and Liabilities of Domestically Chartered Commercial Banks in the United States;
Solvency ratio = risk assets/equity, Liquidity ratio = deposits/cash and reserves.

5.3 Too Big to Fail

Congressional Inquiry into the collapse and bailout of Continental Illinois National Bank

Laeven and Valencia (2012) identify 147 banking crises globally over the period from 1970 to 2011. Central to these systemic banking crises are the policy agendas governments use to re-establish financial stability. Valencia et al. (2008: 3) find it important to recognise that policy decisions that:

> reallocate wealth toward banks and debtors and away from taxpayers face a key trade-off. Such reallocations of wealth can help to restart productive investment, but they have large

> costs. These costs include taxpayers' wealth that is spent on financial assistance and indirect costs from misallocations of capital and distortions to incentives that may result from encouraging banks and firms to abuse government protections. Those distortions may worsen capital allocation and risk management after the resolution of the crisis.

In the United States, where our story is mainly situated, the major systemic crisis to occur between the Great depression and the Great Recession (GFC) was the Savings and Loans crisis of the 1980s and early 1990s. This crisis saw the failure of 3,000 commercial banks and thrifts. This compares to only 243 banks that failed from 1934 to 1980. At a cost of $160 billion to rescue, by 1994 one sixth of federally insured banking institutions had either closed or required federal assistance, impacting 20% of the banking system's assets (FCIC 2011). The case for continued deregulation of banking and finance continued regardless of these failures. This also after the fact that amidst the S&L crisis there had been several major bank bailouts. The common theme being that these banks had funded long term risky loans expansion with volatile and uninsured short-term deposits (FCIC 2010: 36). This is precisely the toxic formula that Simons, Knight and Fisher were concerned with in the 1930s. We deal here with the bailout of the seventh largest bank in the U.S., Continental Illinois National Bank in 1984. The Congressional Report into this bank bailout follows since it provides substantial background information into both the path that a conservative institution can lay towards its own demise, and the accommodative nature of the regulatory oversight that should have foreseen and forestalled such an event.

5.3.1 The Continental Illinois National Bank Bailout

Continental Illinois National Bank (CINB) began to experience liquidity pressures in May 1984. In what Alford would describe as a solvency shock morphing into a liquidity shock, CINB's deteriorating loan book was beginning to disquiet its short-term depositors and investors. The Bank found that its providers of short and term funding were not renewing their holdings, and the Bank was at the same time obliged to prepay time deposits in the Eurodollar markets as well as domestically. Essentially the Bank found that its only source of funds was from the Federal Reserve Bank, its borrowings from which had risen to around $2.6 billion on an average daily basis. On 18 September 1984 a Congressional Inquiry (St Germain 1984) was convened into the rescue of Continental Illinois National Bank (CINB). As the seventh largest bank in America at the time, with assets totalling over $44 billion, the near collapse of CINB was the largest banking crisis since the Great Depression. In his opening remarks the chair of the inquiry, Fernand St Germain said:

> Overall, this case presents an unfortunate combination of aggressive, decentralized management and timid regulatory approaches. There is no more volatile mixture in banking than aggressive management and timid regulation (St Germain 1984: 4).

The total rescue of CINB amounted to over $15 billion. It comprised direct support through the Federal Deposit Insurance Corporation (FDIC) purchasing bad loans from CINB of $4.5 billion plus a further injection of capital totalling $1 billion.[94] Later that year, in August 1984 the Federal Reserve's discount window had lent the bank $7.2 billion and finally, at the urging of federal regulators commercial banks lent CINB $4 billion. The decision by management to turn what had previously been a conservative bank into a major player in the city through aggressive expansion of its loan book had failed. And as St Germain caustically alluded to, it also seems that CINB's senior management failed miserably in expanding its supervision of the bank's internal controls and capacity to accommodate such a rapid increase in its risk assets. Essentially the bank compromised quality for quantity when it came to meeting its expansionary loans targets.

In comparison to the $15 billion bailout of CINB, the Chrysler, Lockheed and New York City bailouts earlier on in the 1970s only amounted to a total of $6 billion dollars (St Germain 1984: 9, 628). But it was not just the size of the comparable bailouts but also how they were managed. St Germain strongly criticised the fact that with the corporate bailouts there had been extensive Congressional debate on the issue of their rescue. However, with the bailout of CINB it was literally done behind closed doors by the regulators and Congress was advised afterwards. In its submission to the Inquiry one of the regulators, the Comptroller General (St Germain 1984: 629), described the necessary process for the rescuing of a significant financial organisation. Unlike the corporate rescues, the CINB bailout had to proceed quickly and in secrecy to avoid a general run of its deposits and an immediate collapse of the bank. The business model of CINB, as with all banks, relies upon the availability of short-term funding to maintain its long-term assets. These depositors and short-term creditors of the bank hold no particular allegiance to it. If there was a sense of increased instability and uncertainty with the bank, they would simply withdraw their funds and deposit them with a safer bank. Furthermore, the repercussions of a failed large banking institution were different and less predictable than those of a failed large corporation. The potential damage caused through its vast array of relationships on a global basis with other banks was incalculable. There was also the potential for a general deterioration of banking confidence and the lessons learnt from the Great Depression meant that this had to be avoided at all costs. This is why Congress delegated 'responsibility for making these determinations to the bank regulatory agencies' (St Germain 1984: 630).

The Congressional Inquiry was equally critical however, not only of the bank's management, but also the regulatory bodies tasked with bank supervision, the Federal Deposit Insurance Corporation (FDIC) and the Office of the Comptroller of the Currency (OCC). We saw in chapter 3 that Henry Simons saw the failure of the system that had led to the Great depression was due to a lack of regulatory oversight and control by the state (Simons 1948: 55). Simons was prepared to allow the state full ownership of the money creating powers currently owned as a monopoly by the banking industry. Minsky was aware of this when he wrote that:

> …the institutional changes which took place as a reaction to the Great Depression and which are relevant to the problem at hand spelled out the permitted set of activities as well as the fiduciary responsibilities of various financial institutions and made the lender of last resort functions of the financial authorities more precise.' (Minsky 2016 (1982): 24)

According to Minsky the failure of the Federal Reserve to act appropriately to curb the banking crisis which spilled into a depression in the 1930s, spurred the American administration under the auspices of the New Deal banking acts to allocate lender of last resort (LOLR) powers to other bodies (Minsky 2016: 24). As such the FDIC with its insurance of bank retail deposits could be seen as further support in times of banking crises. The creation of the Federal Deposit Insurance Corporation (FDIC) was an offshoot of the passing of the Glass Steagall Act in 1933 by Congress. The government now had 'skin in the game' since the FDIC would install confidence in banking via its protection of deposits up to $2,500 initially. This protection grew to $100,000 by 1980 and then was increased to $250,000 during the GFC.

Minsky's thinking is reflected in Figure 5.3.1, where risk assets as represented by the Dow Jones Industrial Average are shown with nominal GDP as a drawdown chart.[95] As can be seen both indicators had a sharp and prolonged fall during the years of the Great depression. However, post that period, even though risk assets had substantial falls in the mid 1970s and during the GFC in 2007/08, these falls were short lived and there was no meaningful fall in GDP. Scaled on the right-hand index we show the growth in M2 money supply over the same period. It can be seen as a curve rising to the right exponentially. Is there a correlation between rising liquidity and the lack of deep and long-lasting asset drawdowns as Minsky suggests?

Figure 5.3.1 Risk Assets and GDP drawdowns compared to growth in M2

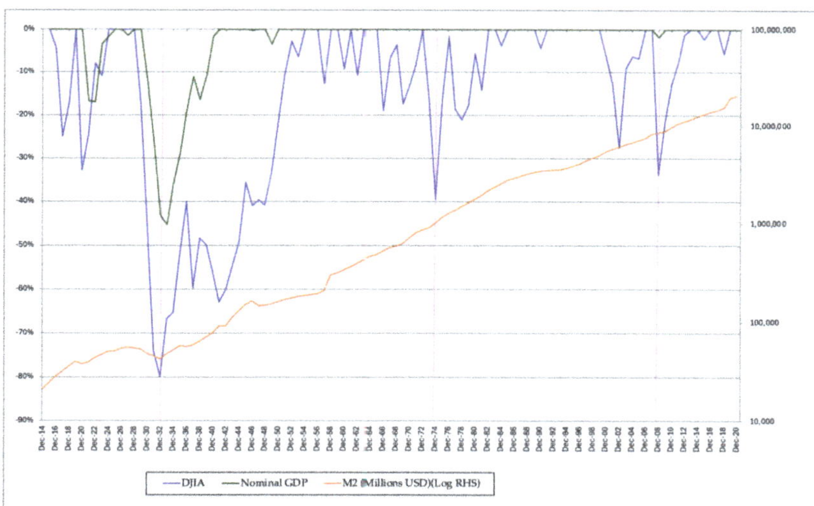

Source: GDP: https://fred.stlouisfed.org/series/GDP; M2: https://fred.stlouisfed.org/series/M2NS; DJIA: Samuel H. Williamson, 'Daily Closing Value of the Dow Jones Average, 1885 to Present,' Measuring Worth, 2021; Drawdown calculation by author.

It was the combination of this additional LOLR coverage provided by the FDIC, combined with a much more assertive Federal Reserve that was much more prepared to add liquidity as required, that put a floor on business cycles post 1966 since due to this enhanced support asset values did not fall as much as during the 1930s (Minsky 2016: 18). But here we arrive at a conundrum. If it becomes apparent to banks that downside risk is limited due to the availability of regulatory support, then why would not the rational investor pile on more risk? In fact, they did as will be shown in the next section.[96] Not only has banking and finance increased its risk taking, but also the Federal Reserve (as with all other central banks) continues to ensure that asset values do not fall, because of the liquidity crises caused by this increased risk taking. The renewed mentality was that asset prices had to be supported at all costs to prevent a repeat of the Great depression.

5.3.2 Too big to fail …again, and again, and…

The Congressional Committee member Stewart McKinney, the Representative from Connecticut, was also highly critical of both Bank management and the regulators that were supposed to supervise them. In the Inquiry report (St Germain 1984) McKinney questions Bank management's ability to manage a loan portfolio. If they cannot do that he continues, then how can they be trusted to manage insurance, securities or mortgage portfolios. He refers to a similar inquiry held two years prior into the failure of Penn Square Bank from Oklahoma and questions how CINB, in light of that collapse could similarly grow its loan book so excessively without regulators sounding the alarm.[97] There are continued echoes of the arguments posed in the 1930s by Frank Knight and Henry Simons regarding the inability of banks to manage their long term fixed assets appropriately. As they wrote not only was the leverage too high in relation to equity, but their dependence on short term liabilities to fund those assets was highly risky. McKinney asserts that after the Chrysler and New York bailouts no major corporation or city has emerged also seeking to be bailed out because of the stringent oversight conditions imposed. However, in banking the administrators are happy to bailout failures without recourse to the people paying the bills. McKinney then coins the famous phrase 'Too Big to Fail' when he says:

> I would also like to find out what the regulators feel they have done, No. 1, by creating a new class of bank in the United States of America, a TBTF—too big to fail. (St Germain 1984: 89).

One of the original contributors to the Chicago Plan memorandum of 1933, Albert G. Hart, contributed to the CINB Congressional inquiry through a submission on the potential for FDIC reform. Hart observed that many other banks like CINB would display weaknesses due to the instability of their deposits base. It is because of this instability that the Roosevelt government created the Federal Deposit Insurance Corporation in the 1930s. But as we have already shown, and as Hart states in his submission, bank aggressiveness in the expansion of its loan portfolios, funded primarily through short term deposit liabilities, would continue to almost guarantee continued banking distress in the future. In this situation regulators like the FDIC find it almost impossible to foretell bank weaknesses in their assets books ahead of crisis developing. Once a crisis occurs, Hart continues, the FDIC is correct to act in a quick and determined manner. There are other policy suggestions proposed by Hart, such as ensuring that large depositors are not guaranteed by the FDIC so that it will be in their interest to ensure the bank is prudently managed. Or increasing the minimum leverage ratio to 10% of equity. Hart however did not think regulators would have the power (nor the fortitude) to enforce such an increase in capital. Hart's solution to banking crises were well documented in his participation with the submission of the Chicago Plan to the Roosevelt administration back in 1933. That conviction appears to continue as he wrote in his submission to the CINB inquiry:

> To fulfil these objectives, and to clean up the risky situation where hundreds of billions of claims not now regarded as part of the money supply can be instantly monetized at the will of the holders, it is desirable also to reform the structure of reserve requirements and the rules applying to quasi-banking institutions. But to keep a sharp focus on FDIC, I leave these problems aside. (St Germain 1984: 614).

It is not explicit in his submission, but was Hart referring to 100% reserves banking as a possible solution to continued banking crises? Next, we move onto the early 21st century and another much bigger financial crisis and another Congressional Inquiry into its causes.

5.4 The GFC - echoes from the past, a thirst for liquidity

The liberation that occurred for the financial system from the late 1970s on was the starting gun for a free for all foray into financial speculations of every description, aided and leveraged to the extreme using derivatives. In the thirty years from 1978 to 2007 financial sector debt increased from $3 trillion to $36 trillion, more than doubling as a share of GDP (FCIC 2011: xvii). The ten largest U.S. Commercial banks increased their assets to 55% of the industry's, again more than doubling from 1990. Financial sector profits reached 27% of total corporate profits in 2006, up from 15% in 1980 (FCIC xvii). The major Wall Street firms had joined in this profit fest as they changed from conservative private partnerships to publicly traded corporations taking greater and greater risk. All this exuberance was channelled into the U.S. housing market with trillions of dollars embedded in risky mortgage structures. Eventually the bubble finally burst as the mortgage market peaked in 2006 and with the demise of one of the largest investment banks,

Lehman Brothers, in September 2008. Much has been written about the events and repercussions of this crisis, but for our purposes here I want to connect with its historic legacy. The aim being to demonstrate that the making of this crisis, those of the past as well as those of the future, all have a genesis in the fact that long term assets are funded with self-created short-term liabilities. It is a contradiction endogenous to the system as constituted today, and as explained by Henry Simons (1948) Hyman Minsky (1992) and many others.

5.4.1 Echoes from the past

Professor Edwin Seligman (Columbia 1908 - see chapter 2) wrote about the monetising of future income streams through the issuance of short-term credit (bank deposits). According to his writing, from time-to-time over-exuberance on the part of entrepreneurs would lead to the overcapitalisation of these future income streams and some extraneous event would eventually lead to the implosion of these structures as everyone headed for the sanctuary of cash. One hundred years later Donald Kohn, Vice Chairman Board of Governors of the Federal Reserve System, wrote in 2010 about just such an event, this time from the point of view of the regulator, the Federal Reserve Bank. A reading of Kohn's paper infers that extraneous events led to the GFC, in other words Kohn's thinking was attuned to Seligman's and the broader banking school of thought. As alluded to in chapter 4 Charles Goodhart (2017) also seems to think that the banks' modern role is that of a service provider. He writes that it is erroneous to consider that banks are solely responsible for the creation of the money supply through the issuance of loans. He absolves the banking industry from the responsibility for the excessive increase and then decrease of the money supply and as such influencing the business cycle. Goodhart places the responsibility for that on the lap of the borrower. He writes:

> Rather than claim that banks create credit, and then such loans create money, it would be much nearer the truth to say that the private sector creates credit and money for itself, and that the banking sector is the medium through which private sector clients do so, on the terms and conditions set out by the banks.(Goodhart 2017: 43)

Hyman Minsky would not have agreed. For Minsky, unlike Seligman and Kohn, but like the currency school beliefs of Simons, Knight and Fisher, the cause for the crisis would have been an endogenous one (Minsky 1957, 1964, 2016). The exuberant over expansion of the bank balance sheet through the expansion of risk assets in relation to equity would cumulatively expose the economy to a systemic financial shock, as reality eventually prevailed in relation to over extended asset valuations. Invariably these risk assets are funded by short term deposits and borrowings which would very quickly be withdrawn, as the solvency shock migrated to a liquidity shock and the availability of short-term funding disappears (see chapter 4). This would lead to a contraction of lending by banks and thus the money supply, sucking the air out of the economy. This was the core issue raised by knight, Simons and Fisher in the 1930s as well as by the Congressional Inquiry into the collapse of CINB in 1984. The Inquiry believed that the CINB had expanded its loan book too aggressively, a management decision which eventually led to the disappearance of its funding sources as the market started to become aware of CINB's perilous financial position. The deterioration of its solvency ratio sparked a run on its liquidity causing the collapse in its liquidity ratio and the necessity for the LOLR bailout by the regulators. And it is precisely, as we will soon see, what occurred because of the Great Financial Crisis over 2007/09.

Minsky (1957) understood well and early the interplay between the regulatory and the market-based institutions. As he wrote the central bank's effectiveness in influencing monetary policy was continuously challenged by the extent of the evolution of banking and functioning of the financial markets. Sometimes after a period of rapid change in financial market development, banks would be ahead of the central bank at which point it would need to adapt. Donald L. Kohn, Vice Chairman of the Board of Governors of the Federal Reserve System admitted as much in a speech he gave fifty years later in 2010, outlining the effectiveness of the FED in supporting the financial markets post GFC. He detailed in his speech:

> Why couldn't the Federal Reserve maintain its routine lending practices and rely on lending to commercial banks, which in turn lend to nonbank firms? The reason is that financial markets have evolved substantially in recent decades--and, in retrospect, by more than we had recognized prior to the crisis. (Kohn 2010: 4)

Kohn goes on to detail the great shift in finance where the intermediation between savers and borrowers has migrated from the commercial bank as the conduit to a market in securities where borrowers and lenders could interact directly, albeit at times through the formation of a new entity - the shadow bank. The development of these securities markets saw the displacement of what used to be bank loans to off balance sheet entities through a process of securitisation.

5.4.2 The shadow banks emerge

The groundswell for the growing deregulation of the financial markets may be put down to the evolutionary prowess of finance to seek its highest return. The inflationary push in the 1960s put upside pressure on interest rates. Banks at the time were hampered by Regulation Q[98] which placed a cap on the interest they could pay depositors, allowing competition from investment banks and funds such as Merrill Lynch, Fidelity and Vanguard. These institutions, with their ability to pay higher deposits, lured deposits away from the banks. These funds were structured as money market Mutual Funds and their business grew from $3 billion in 1977 to more than $740 billion in 1995 and $1.8 trillion in 2000 (FCIC 2010: 30). To maintain their competitive edge these funds sought secure assets to invest in and gradually began to dominate the commercial paper and repo markets. Thus, was seen the onset of a parallel financial market to the banks. This 'shadow market' could provide cheaper financing through commercial paper and repo markets and also provide higher interest on deposits through the money market mutual funds. Banks clamoured and complained to the regulators that they were not able to compete with this shadow market, and regulators in turn were becoming alarmed at the banks' eroding competitive position. This process of 'disintermediation' (Mehrling 2011) eventually led to the full repeal of what was left of the Glass Steagall Act in November 1999. The banks had lobbied strongly for this to occur. As the following excerpt from the Financial Crisis Inquiry Commission (FCIC) report (2010: 55) shows, the banking lobby was, and is, able to bring considerable lobbying power to bear on politicians and regulators:

> In 1999, the financial sector spent $187 million lobbying at the federal level, and individuals and political action committees (PACs) in the sector donated $202 million to federal election campaigns in the 2000 election cycle. From 1999 through 2008, federal lobbying by the financial sector reached $2.7 billion; campaign donations from individuals and PACs topped $1 billion.

The origin of the 'shadow-banking' system described by Mehrling (2011: 82) was also in the advent of the swap and securitisation markets in the 1980s and 1990s. It was an opportunity to shift assets and liabilities off the bank balance sheet and allow banks to fly under the radar of the regulatory institutions. As Mehrling wrote this led to the development of a capital market-based system that grew to be a more important source of credit than traditional banking. However as much as shadow banks may have appeared a successful conduit for increasing the potential for profit through financial engineering, this new and increasing means of profiteering couldn't abstract way from the reality of the need for liquidity. As Mehrling puts it one day you have a nice risk portfolio earning a steady return funded by short term or overnight borrowings and the next your funding disappears, and you can't sell your assets to reduce gearing (Mehrling 2011: 92). The trick of course is knowing when to get out before everyone else starts to head for the exits. The old adage being that when the music stops, you had better be able to find a chair. The market however had, and has, become accustomed to the authorities obligingly coming to the party with a fresh supply of chairs. This systematic bias towards providing liquidity by the authorities has been put to good use by risk takers (Mehrling 2011: 91).

In fact, the core disruption leading to the GFC, as was the case with the Great Depression, was the disappearance of liquidity. Regardless of what the liquidity was destined to fund. In the end as Kohn (2010: 3) says:

> disruptions to financing markets posed the same threats to the availability of credit to households and businesses that runs on banks created in the more bank-centric financial system of the 1800s and most of the 1900s.

Mehrling (2011: 136) also believed that the financial crisis of 2007/09 resonated with earlier financial crises when he said:

> On the eve of the Fed's centennial year, we find ourselves grappling with many of the same issues that concerned

> the Fed's founders albeit not with the benefit of a century's experience with central banking American style.

Kohn and Mehrling agree that the old fashion style of banking where depositors and borrowers meet through a bank has changed to a market-based process where they meet through securities. This evolution has probably occurred to 1) remove lending from bank balance sheets and 2) avoid regulatory impediments (Kohn 2010: 4; Mehrling 2011: 113). This evolution of finance somehow implies that bank liquidity requirements are no longer 'hostage' to having a required, and low earning holding of cash liquidity. It seemed that in the lead up to the GFC (and any other financial crisis) it wasn't the fear of Mrs Jones banging on the counter for her money, rather it was the necessity to fund the loans that had been securitised. It was the need for short term liquidity to fund the calls on previously promised funds to investment banks. It was the need to fund the market.

5.4.3 The GFC - a thirst for liquidity

Liquidity requirements today are vastly different to liquidity requirements in Bagehot's days as Mehrling (2011) suggests. He reasons that in accordance with the changes in the need for liquidity, that the central bank also needs to adapt from being "'lender of last resort" to the more appropriate modern conception of it as "dealer of last resort"' (Mehrling 2011: 114). His rationale being that finance has moved on from the real bills doctrine of self-liquidating debts to the contemporary 'shiftability of securities in liquid markets' (Mehrling 2011: 114). As Mehrling explains liquidity, in the midst of this transformation from bank intermediation to market intermediation, has not in fact become a 'free good' (Mehrling 2011: 136). The question therefore that arises for Mehrling is how the central bank is to manage the liquidity needs of this new way of doing things, both in normal as well as in crisis times. This is the very question posed by Kohn (2010) and was the same question that plagued the central bank during the 1930s. Liquidity seems to be something that is not that important, until it is.

Since the modern financial system is built on a system of split circuit banking (chapter 6 deals with this in detail), banks and other authorised depository institutions are the only ones that have access to the optimum liquidity, in the form of high-level central bank money. This is the liquidity that all participants aspire to in times of crisis, including households, as well as businesses albeit they can only obtain it via their account with a bank or authorised depository institution. In reading Mehrling's (2011) 'The New Lombard Street' one gets a sense that the role of the central bank is to bail out the market when it needs it. Initially it was to allow for the agricultural cycles that would from time to time drain available liquidity. That has now become a necessity to rescue excessive market incursions into exotic financing structures that implode from time to time, in order to rescue present value structures that have enriched a few elites. Is the central bank gifting the present value of doubtful future value income streams to market participants? The wanton expansion of the bank balance sheet, and its implications for the growth and subsequent contraction of the money supply, was the core issue raised in the Chicago Plan for Banking Reform and 100% money during the 1930s. It is also the central issue of the Sovereign Money Creation movement today, as we will now see.

5.5 Conclusion

Chapter 5 moved forward in time from the Great Depression to the Great Financial Crisis. We saw in Section 5.2 the evolution of two distinct economic ears. The Golden Years of Capitalism remained under tight regulatory controls imposed during the Great Depression years. This was in line with the thinking of Henry Simons and the other scholars supporting the Chicago Plan. The state, by playing a dominating part in the functioning of finance, was able to maintain the 'rules of the game' and the subsequent discipline imposed on the banks ensured that debt was directed towards production. In section 5.2 substantial empirical analysis showed the divergences in the growth of bank assets and liquidity. These were compared to total debt, consumption and risk assets. A series of Base 1000 indices were constructed to best reflect not the absolute level of these data points, but their relative rates of change in cumulative growth. We saw how under the 'Great moderation' where the free market became the sole arbiter for financial innovation, that debt to GDP increased from1.5:1 to nearly 4:1 over the Neoliberal period. Concurrently there was an increase in risky assets as shown by the DJIA and a flattening in economic growth as shown by GDP whilst the bank liquidity ratio more than halved in value. We conclude that left to their own devises the banking and shadow banking industries run a constant risk of over gearing in their pursuit of greater profits. The net result being one of financial crisis and the subsequent expected bailout by the public purse.

Well before the events of 2007/09 there had been many opportunities for the authorities to learn from the excesses of a banking institution. Section 5.3 detailed the collapse of Continental Illinois National Bank, the seventh largest bank in America. In 1984, it was the largest banking upheaval since the great depression, but soon to be surpassed by the Savings and Loans crisis. Regulators were forced to inject $15 billion to rescue the institution from fear of the unknown impacts on the wider system. This event led to Representative Stewart McKinney to coin the term 'Too Big To Fail' in reference to the fact that regulators would always bail out a banking institution for fear of such impacts. The Congressional Inquiry into this bank's collapse was highly critical of the regulatory failure in monitoring CINB's growing risk assets and alerting the authorities in advance of the collapse of their misgivings. This was a warning, a shot across the bows of what can happen when aggressive banking meets timid regulation.

In section 5.4 we saw that as Mehrling (2011) and Kohn (2010) wrote there are fundamental similarities between the two financial crises. Both crises, albeit for different reasons, saw a contraction of liquidity which threatened the existing structures and institutions of their times. It seems that regardless of the synthesising of future income streams to provide present value, there is always an unavoidable arbiter called liquidity, which brings excesses to account. So that the continued pursuit of maturity transformation, where long term illiquid loans are supported by short term on demand liabilities continues to ensure the fragility in bank balance sheets. Simons, Knight and Fisher wrote about this extensively in the 1930s. Even if Bagehot's 'lender of last resort' transforms into Mehrling's 'dealer of last resort' there is no getting away from the suspicion that central banks are seeking the illusive power of alchemy to 'invent liquidity'. As the growth in central bank balance sheets has shown however, the end result is not the transformation of lead into gold, but the transformation of private losses into public losses.

Chapter 6

Second Debate on Monetary Reform: Sovereign Money Creation

6.1: Introduction

Chapter 6 looks at the second major debate on monetary reform, Sovereign Money Creation (SMC). Firstly, in section 6.2 we rely on Joseph Huber's depiction of our contemporary monetary regime as being a split circuit system. That is, there are two types of money, central bank money and commercial bank money.[99] As we will show, households and non-financial businesses only have limited access to central bank money via actual currency notes. This only makes up as very small percentage of the total money supply (3% to 10%), with the remainder being digital deposits created by banks when they issue loans. Although Central bank money is the favoured repository of wealth, especially during financial crises, there is only limited access to it since the banking industry sits ponderously between it and client wealth. And it does so whilst reaping substantial profits from it. Huber proposes a single circuit monetary system that removes this interference by the banks and provides direct access to central bank money by households and businesses. The banks are relegated to being service providers for this type of money. Although they are still able to issue loans and pay interest on time deposits, they cannot generate their own deposits. As we will see Huber's proposed SMC system differs from the Chicago Plan and Fisher's 100% Money through important structural procedures. Primarily, fractional reserves banking is entirely removed. Unlike the Chicago Plan banks would not have the capacity to create money first and seek reserves to fund it later. There is only one type of money - sovereign money.

In Section 6.3 *Sovereign inquiries into monetary reform*, we look at enquiries held by three countries, the USA, Iceland and Switzerland, all prompted by, and post the Great financial Crisis (GFC) of 2007/09. There were many more countries that investigated the possibility of monetary reform but these three provide a good example of a broad attempt that did not make to Congressional debate (USA), an inquiry prompted by a parliamentary statute (Iceland) and an inquiry that made it to a peoples' referendum (Switzerland). We will look at the results of these inquiries and at the movements for monetary reform that have grown across the world. All three inquiries have connections to the Chicago Plan inquiry of the 1930s. Once again, a financial crisis focuses debate on the stability of the medium of exchange. These three inquiries into monetary reform are adamant that the financial system would benefit from a single circuit monetary paradigm. This would remove the risks to the broader economy that excessive risk taking, promoted by excessive lending by the banking industry, invariably produces. All three enquiries however failed to be enacted into law. The Swiss referendum in particular saw an overt and very large campaign against the proposed monetary reforms mounted by the established financial industry, including the Swiss National bank.

Section 6.4 Central Bank Digital Currencies briefly assesses research being carried out by governments and central banks into providing direct access to central bank money to the household and non-financial industry. Initially it appeared that the vast improvements in block chain technology would provide the means for the central bank to manage this transfer from commercial bank deposits to central bank digital deposits. Here was a mechanistic solution to Huber's proposal for a single circuit monetary system. The discussions are not finalised, but it does appear however that central banks are approaching this from a payments system point of view rather than a sovereign money solution. This seems apparent since commercial banks would still be allowed to create deposits through loans under a CBDC system. Also, other private digital currencies known as 'stable coin' are being considered. There is considerable concern amongst central banks as well about the impact of commercial bank funding if customers are given the option to transfer their savings to a digital deposit account with the central bank. Discussions are ongoing but it does seem that there is now the why, as well as the means for a sovereign money system. All that is missing according to Huber (2019) is the will.

6.2 Sovereign Money Creation

There are important differences and similarities between the Chicago Plan push for 100% reserves banking in the 1930s and the Sovereign Money Creation (SMC) being promoted today. One adjoining factor however is the currency school principle that the creation of money should be entirely separate to the intermediation of money. Both schemes also promote the issuance of the medium of exchange by a government constituted body so that the state can regain control over the money supply and the seigniorage benefits attached to that.[100] When we left those debates however at the end of chapter 3, we had good arguments as to why those proposals should have been implemented by president Roosevelt as part of the New Deal proposals, but we did not have a solution as to how. Apart from the enormous 'push back' by the banks, on a technical basis the implementation of 100% reserves would have found it difficult to accomplish its objectives due to the operational difficulties in managing a reserves-based system. 'Reserves' in this system is the term for primary, or central bank money of account. It refers to money accessible only to banks through their accounts with the central bank and it is the means that banks use to settle accounts between themselves (See Huber 2015). The transactions between banks and non-banks and between non-banks and other non-banks is by means of secondary, or bank money. These two flows of money never intermingle. Non-banks do not have access to the central bank accounts and money, and bank-to-bank transactions cannot be settled using customer deposits.

6.2.1 Split Circuit Banking

Non-bank clients interact with the money supply through debtor/creditor relations with the banks. Money transactions between these customers occurs through bank on demand deposit accounts. Figure 6.2.1 reflects this flow. Just to recap what has already been said, the bank creates a deposit on the allocation of a loan to the client. When the client draws these funds and transacts with their clients who bank with a different bank, the initiating bank interacts with the recipient bank through its reserves account with the central bank (see Figures 4.3.2 and 4.3.3 above).[101] The flows of interbank reserves and on demand customer bank money never mingle. This is a split circuit of banking, and it is the financial regime under which modern society functions (Huber 2015, 2017, Dyson et al. 2016). This is the corner stone of the system under which society has developed since the 1930s. This system has become even further entrenched than when Frank D. Graham wrote nearly one hundred years ago:

> the social implications of the private issue of money have thus grown more obscure, though not less vital, as we have become inured to the present practice... (Graham 1936: 440).

That is, it is difficult for society to encompass and alternate way of things in regard to money. We try and demonstrate such an alternative below.

Figure 6.2.1 Split circuit reserve banking

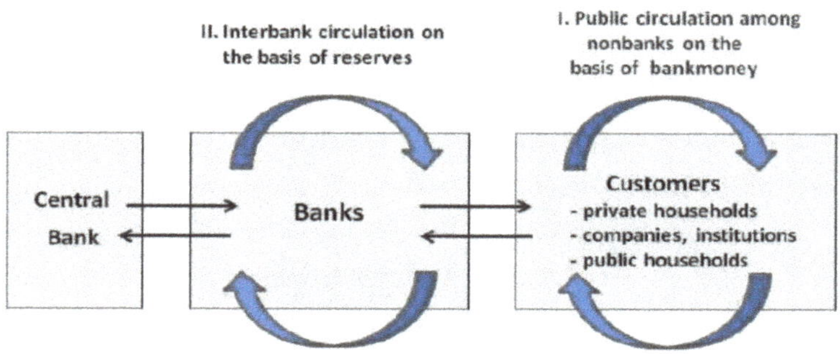

Source: Huber 2017: 64

There is a third circuit which is the notes and coin currently produced by the sovereign. However as has already been discussed this mode of exchange is now a small fraction of the total money supply with 95% of transactions occurring through bank money. Banks would like nothing better than to fully disperse with this 'nuisance' mode of exchange settlement and it can be safely discarded in our discussion here (Huber 2015: 6, 2017: 65).

Daily banks go through a process of clearing liabilities against each other and arriving at a net reserves surplus or deficit. The surplus banks would normally lend reserves to the deficit banks and in situations where this does not occur (as during a liquidity crunch such as the GFC or when the system as a whole has a reserves deficit), the central bank would step in under the lender of last resort facility. The 100% reserves proposals put by the Chicago scholars and others seem to imply that although the central bank, or some other government instituted body[102] would be responsible for ensuring that banks maintained $1 in reserves for every $1 in deposit liabilities, that the system would remain a split circuit system. That is the banks would continue to issue loans as on demand deposit liabilities and then seek to bulk up the required reserves to the 100% coverage required (Huber 2015). These additional reserves would be issued by the prescribed government authority either through the purchase of government debt held by the banks, or where there is not enough government debt to cover 100% deposit liabilities, through the purchase of secondary debt.[103] The government could also lend the reserves to the banks as well. However, the full 100% reserves are arrived at, and even if there is no interest cost to the bank, it would still be in the form of debt. The reserves could not be lent directly to the client; the passage of money would still be two tiered. That is, from the central bank to the bank, and then from the bank to the customer. Here Huber (2015: 6) raises the question as to why we need to:

> continue with the split process of clearing of deposits (bank liabilities) and settlement of the balance in reserves (liquid central-bank assets); instead of doing the clearing and settlement in just one kind of money, i.e. fully available central-bank money?

The not-for-profit advocacy group Positive Money,[104] based in London, was formed in 2010 mainly because of the role that money and banking played in the 2007/09 financial crisis, and the fact that no one was talking about it. According to their website their mission statement strives for 'a money and banking system that enables a fair, democratic, and sustainable economy.' Dyson et al. (2016) lays out Positive money's approach to developing a new monetary system. It relies on Huber (2015) largely in that it also promotes reverting from a split circuit to a single circuit monetary system. Positive Money believes that the 100% reserves system previously promoted by Irving Fisher and the Chicago Plan has structural and mechanistic problems that may explain why such a system was not taken up. For example, since the 100% full reserves system still operates on a two-tier basis, central bank reserves are still drawn upon in support of on demand deposits. That however would not impede the banking system continuing to issue on demand deposits as loans and then seeking the required reserves from the central bank. Why not then just give people direct access to the central bank money and avoid the middle step of going through the bank? Dyson et al. (2016: 27) write:

> In contrast, in a full sovereign money system there would be only one integrated quantity of money circulating among banks and non-banks alike. In effect, the public would be able to make its payments using central bank reserves directly, rather than having to use bank deposits.

6.2.2 Single Circuit Banking

Under a Sovereign Money Creation system banks are removed as the originator and eventual owner of client money. There is no complicated clearing process as occurs with fractional or 100% reserves banking. There no longer would exist a two-tiered system of central bank reserves money only used by banks, and bank money to be used by non-banks. There would no longer be different classes of money supply such as Base, M1, M2 or M3 (see Huber 2015). Figure 6.2.2 demonstrates the flow of money under SMC. There is only one type of money which always remains the property of one owner, until disposed of through exchange.

Figure 6.2.2 Single circuit banking

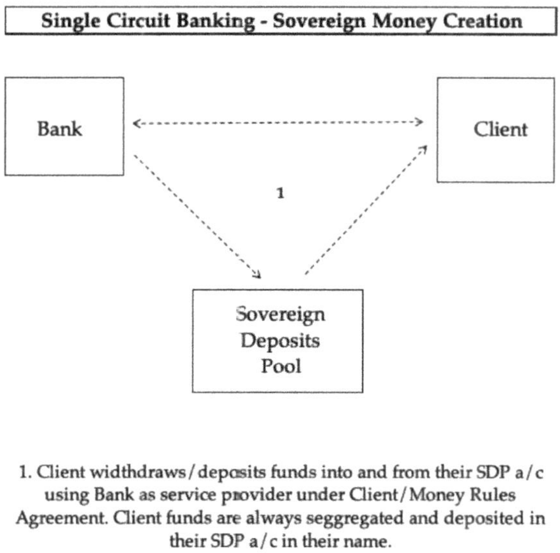

Source: Huber 2015; diagram by author

In this scenario there is no credit risk for on demand deposits like M1. Clients wishing to invest excess funds through M2 or M3 would choose to incur credit and counterparty risk in exchange for a fee or interest payment. Banks would fund themselves through access to these savings, through the accumulation of profits in debt free money and through borrowing from the central authority in case of emergency. They would again become lenders of real funds in a reversion to the actual intermediation between savers and borrowers.

Relying on this author's prior experience as a futures Commodities Trading Advisor an analogy for how such a SMC system might work is the futures clearing system. The centralised clearing system under which the futures market operates has managed to remove financial and credit risk from its operating principles. Traders (be they individuals or corporations) are assessed for their capacity to finance the risk they enter into, and this is monitored on a real time basis. Greater volatility for example, is a requirement for increased margin contributions by the trader. Clearing Member Firms (Futures Brokers) are prohibited from interposing their own balance sheet between traders and the money flows are ensured, under client money rules, in between principals. Unlike the current macroeconomic arrangements that lead to increases and decrease in the money supply, there is no fractional gearing of the margin supplied by clients supporting their trades. For example, brokers in the futures system are not allowed to pool trader margins into their deposit liabilities account and use those funds to make their own investments.

Figure 6.2.3 Sovereign money creation system - functions as single circuit banking

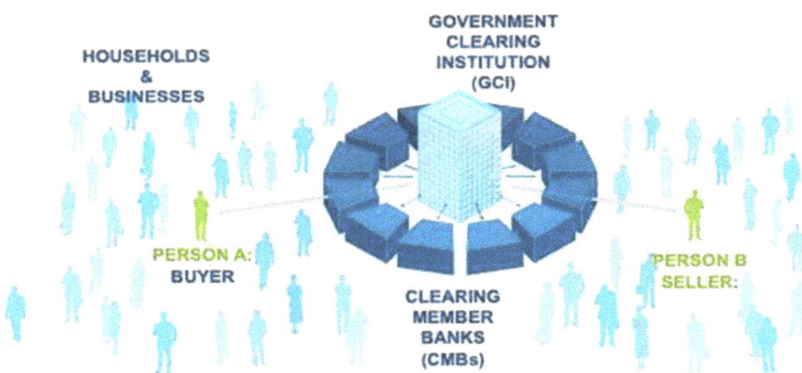

Source: Huber 2015; diagram by author stylised from: FuturesFundamentals.org.

In the stylised diagram above instead of traders A and B we have person A (Buyer) wishing to transact with person B (Seller). The Clearing House member firms would be replaced by new institutions called Clearing Member Banks (CMBs) and the Clearing House would be the Government Clearing Institution (GCI). The GCI would be the transaction clearing and accounting subsidiary of the Government Institution (GI) mandated to issue the fiat money supply. The role of the GI would be mandated through constitutional legislation to ensure independence. In this instance Client A advises their CMB of the intended transaction via some payments process. The CMB in this instance, unlike the current banking institution, does not replace Client A's debt obligation to Client B with its own obligation, as it would under current banking arrangements but instead, would simply be the processor for the payment. The CMB advises the GCI of the transaction. The GCI would debit Client A's account and credit Client B's account to complete the transaction. In this process neither Client A nor Client B incur any credit or counterparty risk with the CMB. The CMB cannot influence the money supply and therefore the economic cycle since it is simply a service provider acting as a conduit between the client and their account with the GCI. Under this SMC system the bank balance sheet is not impacted by the transfer of funds from Client A to Client B. What would change would be the registered ownership of the funds in question.

KPMG & Jourdan (2016) propose a similar clearing arrangement used in current securities clearing as shown below in Figure 6.2.4.

Figure 6.2.4 Securities Clearing as a model for a SMC system.

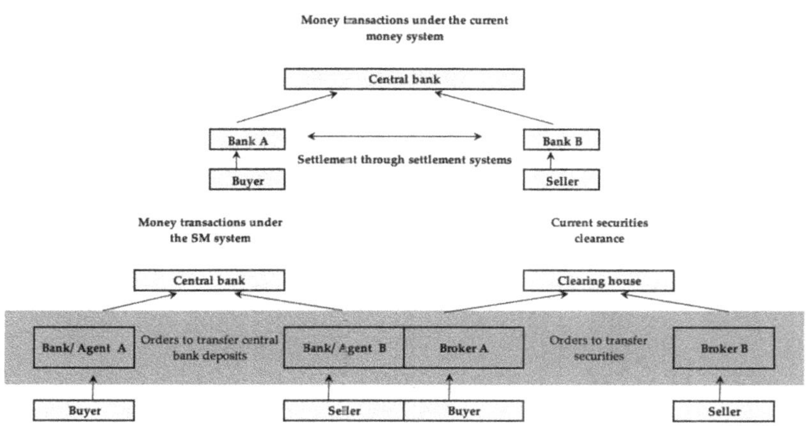

Source: KPMG & Jourdan (2016: 14)

This model is precisely like the futures clearing model discussed above. In this instance, as with a futures clearing system the securities Clearing House would become the Government Institution (central bank?), charged with the holding of the client assets and the administration of the payments systems. The banks become brokers with all client monies protected under client money rules. The factors that stand out are:

1) client funds are always off the bank balance sheet,

2) banks act as clearing agents (brokers) rather than principals,

3) client funds always remain the property of the client through client money rules and the banks are prohibited from pooling these funds into a bulk 'deposits' liability account.

There are many variations and finer details that would need to be ironed out of course. One critical detail not yet discussed is how and under what rules is money to arrive into the system, if not through a bank loan. In the next section we assess three actual proposals put forward for SMC and see how this may work in real time.

6.3: Sovereign inquiries into monetary reform

The Financial Crisis Inquiry Commission (FCIC 2010: 16) report attributed the source of the GFC to:

> the collapse of the housing bubble—fueled by low interest rates, easy and available credit, scant regulation, and toxic mortgages—that was the spark that ignited a string of events, which led to a full-blown crisis in the fall of 2008.

Well before that, if the St Germain Inquiry into the collapse of Continental Illinois National Bank in 1984 was asked to provide an opinion on as to why the GFC occurred they may well have described it as:

> Overall, this case presents an unfortunate combination of aggressive, decentralized management and timid regulatory approaches (St Germain 1984: 4).

Regardless of the why or the how, the fact was that it happened - again. Therefore, various governments around the world held inquiries into the potential for monetary reform to avoid another repetition of the financial destabilisation of the global economy. We will deal with the American, the Icelandic and the Swiss enquiries here. The American since it was the source of the overextended markets. The Icelandic because it was one of the worst affected countries and its Inquiry was at the parliamentary level and the Swiss because the move to change the way money enters the system actually made it to a referendum.

6.3.1 The American Inquiry: The National Emergency Employment Defense (NEED) Act, HR 2990

Up until his untimely death in an aeroplane crash on 6 May 1935 Republican Senator Bronson Cutting was the lead sponsor of a bill in Congress seeking monetary reform. Cutting was greatly influenced by the Chicago Plan and Irving Fisher, who helped him draft the Bill. The aim of the Bill, drafted amongst the chaos of the Great Depression, was to remove from banks the ability to issue money, the medium of exchange, through the issuance of debt. Nearly eighty years later, in a repeat performance and after another financial catastrophe, Democratic Representative Dennis Kucinich introduced a bill into the House on 21 September 2011 seeking similar things. Kucinich,[105] the Representative for Ohio from 1997 to 2013, actively criticised the bailouts given to the banks post GFC. The Bill he proposed was eventually unsuccessful due to lack of support for, and tremendous support against it. James Buchanan, the 1986 Nobel Laureate in Economic Sciences, shared similar sentiments with Kucinich. It is unknown whether Kucinich was influenced by Buchanan but certainly Kucinich's aim was in tune with Buchanan's thinking. Buchanan had been a pupil of Simons and Knight and like his early tutors believed that there was a place for the state in governing aspects of the free market.[106] Burns (2016: 312) writes that Buchanan:

> stridently argued that the core rules governing monetary-financial institutions should be established at the constitutional level of collective decision-making and not at the post-constitutional level where the market game or ordinary politics is played out.

Buchanan's GFC monetary analysis was a 'post monologue' (Burns 2016: 312) of Simons' views expounded in his a 'Positive Program for Laissez Faire' (1934). Basically, Buchanan believed that the 'rules of the game' should be codified at a higher level than the government of the day, 'they should be firmly established at the constitutional level' (Burns 2016: 313).

Buchanan believed that within the 'Hobbesian covenant' security was primal in an anarchistic setting (Buchanan 2010). To that end he wanted to:

> amend Hobbes by extending the umbrella to include money and to do so with the understanding that security is reckoned in the stability and/or predictability in value (Buchanan 2010: 252).

This primordial application of a definition to money as the medium of exchange is very apt. We could hang the hats of all our writers on money so far on this hook.[107] It is the stability and/or predictability in the value of the medium of exchange which is crucial to a fair society. According to Buchanan this fact was so important that money should be managed neither by the free market nor political government. Rather, how money is to be managed should be inscribed at the constitutional level, beyond the reach of politicians and private individuals (Boettke et al. 2018: 536).[108] Buchanan (2010: 256) himself wrote:

> In application to money, the requirement is that the value of the monetary unit be made one of the rules of the game, within which economic interaction takes place, rather than being used as a counter in the strategy of play within the rules

As he extends the argument further (Buchanan 2010: 253), in exchange for the surrender to the sovereign the constitutional right to manage money, society would in return expect the ensuing security that a predictable value in the medium of exchange should offer. We now turn to the NEED Act (H.R. 2990 2011-1012) to see what was put on the Congressional record.

Congressman Kucinich's activism for monetary change via the NEED Act (2010, 2011) was also supported by Kaoru Yamaguchi from Doshisha University and Stephen Zarlenga from the American Monetary Institute. Yamaguchi was invited to speak at a Congressional Briefing organised by Congressman Dennis Kucinich on 26 July 2011 (Yamaguchi 2011). Kucinich was preparing to resubmit his NEED Act Bill and had developed an interest in Yamaguchi's 'macroeconomic simulations on the workings of public money system'. Yamaguchi used a systems dynamics approach to promote a macroeconomic system of 'public money' rather than the existing system of 'debt money' (Yamaguchi 2019: 375, 386). He believed that money was 'always endogenous' and that it 'continues to sit in the center of all macroeconomic behaviors' (Yamaguchi 2019: viii). As a contrast Yamaguchi (2019: viii) wrote that

> Under the Keynesian analytical framework, money has been all the time treated as an adjunct to the macroeconomic system; that is, money has been regarded as an exogenous entity, not as an endogenous one. This may be the reason why employment comes first, followed by interest and money comes last in the title of the book.

Yamaguchi believes that after the Second Great Depression (GFC) that the rebuilding cannot be along the lines of Keynesian government borrowing (deficit funding) (Yamaguchi 2019: 371). This only serves to continue to promote the 'debt money system' since governments will borrow the money from the banks, or from non-banks who in turn borrow from the banks, leading to the banks expanding their balance sheets. Rather Yamaguchi wants to revitalise a modern version of the 100% Reserves proposals of the Chicago Plan and Irving Fisher's 100% Money through the creation of a 'public money system' (Yamaguchi 2019: 372).

At the Congressional Briefing mentioned above Yamaguchi proposed that the debt money system operating until the onset of the GFC could not continue. Rather through the following three features of the NEED Act proposed by Kucinich, and based on the Chicago Plan of the 1930s, a public money system would be imposed (Yamaguchi 2019: 372):

1) Governmental control over the issue of money
2) Abolishment of credit creation with full reserve ratio of 100%
3) Constant inflow of money to sustain economic growth and welfare

Yagamuchi was supported by Stephen Zarlenga who founded the American Monetary Institute[109] and was a proponent of the American Monetary Act (Zarlenga 2010). This Act was reflected in the NEED Act 2010 submitted by Congressman Kucinich in 2010 and 2011. In his 2002 opus the *Lost Science of Money*, Zarlenga lays out his view that money is best served as a creation of law (2002). It therefore needs to be a creation of the state. Money today that exists as a factor of credit, is best served through the banks. In this latter case the growth of debt over the last hundred years has demonstrated its inefficacy. To Zarlenga money can be defined as 'an abstract social power embodied in law, as an unconditional means of payment' (Zarlenga 2002: 657). In accordance with Buchanan's constitutionalism Zarlenga believed that:

> ...ultimately the monetary power should be constituted as a fourth branch of government, like the executive, judicial and legislative branches. We have concluded that the nature of man and of society requires four, not three, branches of government (Zarlenga 2002: 657)

These words could have been spoken by Frederick Soddy, Frank Knight or Irving Fisher who amongst many others, all believed similar things.

In a video[110] interview given early May 2012 Congressman Kucinich lays out the core of his proposed monetary reform bill the NEED Act 2011[111](NEED Act 2011). First, he sets out the core issue as being the fact that banks are the source of the money supply and therefore can wield great power when dealing with government. He questions the bailing out of the banks after the GFC to the tune of trillions of dollars, whilst ordinary Americans have lost their jobs and homes. He lays the problem at the door of Congress for the cessation of the power to create the money supply and the passing it over to the banks and suggests that it must revert to government outlining three steps, all of which were previously laid out by the proponents of the Chicago Plan, required to achieve so:

A) the Federal reserve system is to be subsumed within Treasury where all new money would be issued without debt or interest, adding to revenue with taxing or borrowing and spent into circulation

B) end the practice of fractional reserves lending which allows banks to issue the money supply as interest bearing debt. The aim would be to nationalise the money system not the banking system so that banks would be allowed to lend previously sourced funds but not funds created as a bank liability.

C) new money is spent into circulation as the economy grows.

The NEED Act (NEED Act 2011) itself proceeds to detail how the model proposed in Figure 6.2.4 above might work. Some summary points are:

A) Section 2 (b) (1) Stipulates the creation of a Monetary Authority to maintain a strict control over the money supply to avoid either inflationary or deflationary cycles. It also establishes the Bureau of the Federal Reserve to administer the origination and entry into circulation of United States Money. In figure 6.2.4 above this would be the Government Institution (GI)[112] and it would have a subsidiary called the Government Clearing Institution (GCI) to manage the process.

B) Section 2 (b) (3) would abolish the power of private institutions or individuals to create purchasing power through lending against deposits by means of fractional reserve banking or any other means. In figure 6.2.4 this means that the Clearing Member Banks would replace existing banks as agents processing instructions from the client to the GCI.

C) Section 2 (b) (4) states that new money would enter the system through investment or lending by the sovereign. New money could also enter the system through gifting or lowering of taxes by the sovereign. In Figure 6.2.4 this new money would be created by the GI and disseminated by the central core GCI.

The transition from fractional reserve to sovereign money has always been a point that has needed clarification. In this Bill essentially, as at the effective date all deposit liabilities held by depository institutions would become United States Money in designated transaction accounts as either cash or electronic equivalent. The Bill would effectively extinguish the banks' on-demand liabilities to its customers and these accounts would then be deemed as accounts held as bailment property, in other words the ownership of the accounts would be in the name of the client, the bank acting only as its custodian. They would cease to be an on-balance sheet item for the bank but rather an off-balance sheet account maintained on behalf of the client. The liability would then be repositioned as a liability to the government and being equal in size, the overall balance sheet of the bank would not change.[113] The liability to the government would be repaid as the client paid down their existing loan to the bank.

The Kucinich Bill wanted to deal with the issues raised since the mid nineteenth century by critics of fractional reserve banking. Section 2 (15) of the Bill poses that the ceding of the constitutional power of the sovereign to issue the medium of exchange, and thus manage the purchasing power of the nation has led to:

A) growing and unreasonable concentration of wealth.
B) unbridled expansion of national debt, both public and private.
C) excessive reliance on taxation of citizens for raising public revenues.
D) devaluation of the currency.
E) drastic increases in the cost of public infrastructure investments.
F) record levels of unemployment and underemployment; and
G) persistent erosion of the ability of Congress to exercise its Constitutional responsibilities to provide resources for the general welfare of all the American people.

These issues were put by Kucinich on the floor of the United States Congress in September 2011. All these measures are readily observable and empirically calculable. Furthermore, this occurred amidst the fallout from the worst financial crisis to engulf the U.S. since the great depression. The Bill however was only able to raise one sponsor and did not manage to proceed. It seems that the banking school again, as it did in the 1930s, has been able to conjure the dominant narrative.

6.3.2 The Icelandic Inquiry: Monetary reform - A Better Monetary System for Iceland

Iceland is a small Nordic country with a population of just over 300,000. It is a perfect sample in a concentrated form, of what can happen to a society whose institutions are opened to the neoliberal free market paradigm (Wade et al. 2012: 127). Dimitra Doukas described it as

> ... a history of neoliberal conquest, writ large on a small island nation, compressed into less than thirty years' time (from the founding of the Icelandic Stock Exchange in 1985) (Doukas 2014: 217)

Deregulation and privatisation from the 1990s to the GFC in 2008 generated a period of enormous growth in financialisation and debt. Figure 6.3.1 below shows the growth in bank credit and bank liquidity compared to Notional GDP. Scaled to the right-hand index is the main Icelandic stock index, ICEX.

Figure 6.3.1 Financial volatility in Iceland

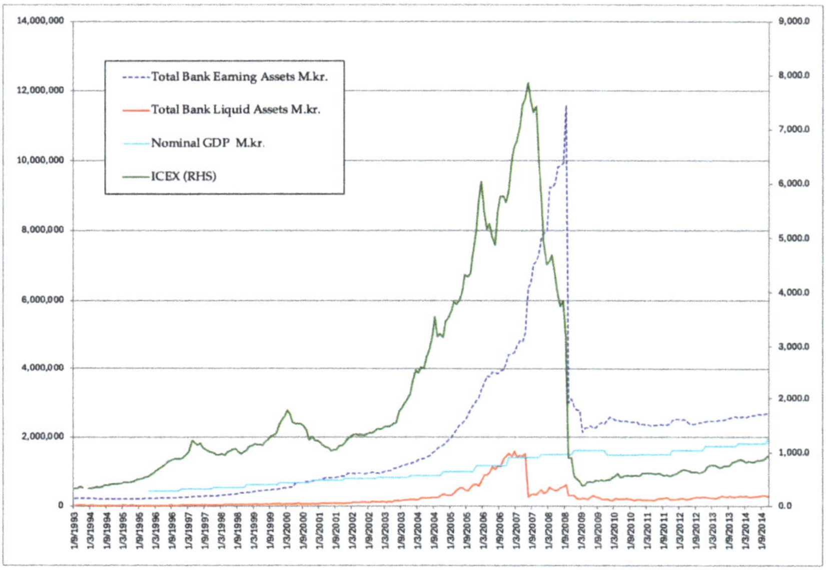

Source: Bank balance sheet data: Central Bank of Ic eland Statistics 'Accounts of deposit taking corporations' - https://www.cb.is/; ICEX: Investing.com - https://au.investing.com/; GDP: Statistics Iceland -https://statice.is/;

It is not just the pace of the rise in financial assets which is striking, but the suddenness of the drop that hit Iceland's economy which is reminiscent of the volatility inferred in a Minsky moment. In considering the economic volatility shown in Figure 6.3.1 it is difficult to connect with Seligman, who wrote in Columbia (1908) that entrepreneurs for some external reason, reassess investments leading to a withdrawal of capital and a contraction. This was obviously not a normal contraction with the ICEX collapsing 95% in less than two years and bank earning assets falling by 82% over a six-month period.

Irving Fisher wrote in his Debt Deflation Theory (1933) that the two 'bad boys' of too much debt combined with asset deflation led to the Great Depression. Knight and Simons highlighted this in their Chicago Plan. The money supply had to be kept stable and as Simons wrote only the state had the power to do so. In his 'Rules Versus Authorities in Monetary Policy' (1936) there were 'rules of the game' that needed to be adhered to in order to maintain stability in the money supply. The extent of the volatility in the speculative ICEX index, as well as in the bank lending numbers clearly demonstrate that the market was wantonly pursuing returns which were not validated or underpinned by production. Table 6.3.1 below shows the highs and lows for the balance sheet measures that Alford would have focused upon.

Table 6.3.1 Extremes of volatility in Icelandic banks (Millions Kr)

	Peak	Valley	Months	High	Low	% Drop
Assets	30/9/08	31/3/09	6	11,593,148	2,140,530	-82%
Liquidity	28/2/07	31/10/10	44	1,597,454	162,058	-90%
Deposits	30/9/08	31/1/13	53	4,312,196	1,599,409	-63%
Capital	30/9/08	31/1/09	4	1,064,259	218,202	-79%

Source: Bank balance sheet data: Central Bank of Iceland Statistics 'Accounts of deposit taking corporations' - https://www.cb.is/;

In an analogy of a bank that finds itself insolvent because it gets ahead of the pack and becomes short on liquidity, Iceland as a very small player found itself extremely overextended, or as Boyes (2009: 2) says 'globalization vaulted it into the economic fast lane'. From the late 1980s to the eventual burst of the balloon in the maelstrom of the GFC, the money supply in Iceland grew at an average of 18.6% p.a. As against its GDP which grew at 3.2% per year (Icelandic Parliament 2016: 3). The Central Bank of Iceland (CBI) raised interest rates from 5.6% in 2004 to 18% in 2008 in an attempt to curb this credit growth to no avail. All that it served to do was to strengthen the Icelandic Krona (ISK) and facilitate the implementation of a carry trade where low interest rate currencies such as the USD or the EUR could be borrowed, exchanged for ISK and placed on deposit there to gain the interest arbitrage. This strategy has been used many times before and usually ends with devastating consequences for the high interest rate currency. This is precisely what happened to the Krona post Lehman crash in 2008 as it was sold off heavily as the hot money was syphoned off from Iceland back to where it originated. The Krona halved in value from 63 ISK to the USD to120 ISK (Icelandic Parliament 2016).

This condition of excessive debt crept up on Iceland, as it did everywhere else in the developed world, almost as a thief in the night. Under the guise of the 'Great Moderation' a decade and a half from 1990 or so seemed to have ushered in a permanency in the existing low and stable inflation and macroeconomic stability (Turner 2016: 31). Under this veil of neutrality for money and its source of origination evolved a 'benign assessment of increasing financial intensity and market liberalisation' (Turner 2016: 31). The banking system, and its impact on the workings of society through its power to generate the medium of exchange as debt, did not figure in the modern macroeconomic modelling. The cacophony of sweetened neoliberal sentiments however can be swamped by the writings of the Old Chicagoans amongst many others, but usually after the fact. They show that the great moderation was in fact a veil for the institutionalisation of the machinery for the extrication of wealth, from the many to the few. As Knight and Simons would attest, this was a failing of the state to ensure the rules of the game were adhered to, in the interests of true libertarian capitalism.

Iceland was one of the few nations to carry out an inquiry at the Parliament (Althingi) sovereign level into the workings of its monetary system. In the Spring of 2015, the Prime Minister of Iceland commissioned Frosti Sigurjonsson to investigate why

Iceland had been so exposed to the financial crisis of 2008. His report (Sigurjonsson 2015) is a comprehensive and detailed report on the negative impacts caused by banks having control of the money supply. It runs to 113 pages and draws upon Soddy, Knight, Simons, Fisher from the early twentieth century and Huber, Turner, King, Dyson and Werner from today, amongst others. Sigurjonsson uses the arguments posed by the Chicago Plan of 1933 to demonstrate the flaws in fractional reserves banking. The amount of money created by the commercial banks was to such an excess that the national currency had lost 99.7% of its value over the 50 years to 2015, Sigurjonsson wrote. Further, he states that this excessive money creation was not done out of ignorance of the consequences, rather it was motivated for a desire for remuneration and profits on behalf of the banks' owners (Sigurjonsson 2015: 61). The variability in the money supply caused through commercial banks excessive lending was specifically mentioned by Frank Knight in his 1927 review of Soddy's 1926 'Wealth, Virtual Wealth and Debt'. In his review (discussed in detail in chapter 3) Knight agrees with Soddy about the 'evils' that result from the 'frightful instability' caused by the variability in the money supply as banks expand and then contract it. In fact, a key question posed by Sigurjonsson is why did the central Bank of Iceland allow the money supply to grow at such an unsupportable pace? After all, as the report says: '*research has shown that rapid growth in the money supply is a crucial clue as to [an imminent] dual crisis, i.e. currency and financial crisis*' (Sigurjonsson 2015: 54, italics in original.) Responses ranged from after the inflation target was achieved the importance of the growth in money supply was ignored, to the CBI did not actually understand what was happening.

Perhaps the more credible explanation, and the one that tends to fit in with what was going on at the global level in finance, was 'that in the fractional reserve system the CBI has no alternative but to provide reserves as needed' (Sigurjonsson 2015: 54). The CBI came to realise as early as 2007 that its three large banks, which had grown in assets to the extraordinary size (for such a small nation) where they ranked amongst the top 300 banks in the world, were in a dangerous risk of failing, and that 'the liquidity provisions from the CBI to the banking system actually constituted emergency lending' (Sigurjonsson 2015: 54). As we have already alluded to the nature of the fractional reserve banking system that reigns today is such that the majority of the money supply enters the system as bank liabilities. As such, the nation's payments system itself is held ransom to the bank's continuing liquidity and to a lesser extent, solvency. Thus, was born the moral hazard concept of the 'too big to fail' bank back in 1984, first uttered by Stewart McKinney during the Congressional Inquiry into the failure of Continental Illinois National Bank (chapter 5). And thus, we see the concomitant need by the banks to have this power to create money. They may well be predominantly large investment companies that exist for the benefits of employees and shareholders, but through the (unlegislated) ability to provide the medium of exchange they have some surety that no matter how reckless their bets, the taxpayer will be there to bail them out in the end.

The Sigurjonsson report made the firm comment that whilst banks had this power to create the medium of exchange as loans that the same risk of occurrence would be in place. The report set out the view of Adair Turner as to the cause of the financial crisis:

> *The financial crisis of 2007/08 occurred because we failed to constrain the private financial system's creation of private credit and money* (Sigurjonsson 2015: 55, italics in original)

Jackson (2013: 4) takes a leaf out of Fisher's (1933) debt deflation theory when he writes that the Great Financial Crisis may well have caused asset prices to collapse, but the amount of the debt incurred in their purchase remained leading to 'a balance sheet recession'.

Further in his report Jackson discusses the question of how the additional creation of money by the state is to be managed under sovereign money creation. In doing so he cannot help but look at the current commercial banking money creation system. Under the current system banks are motivated to expand their money creation because that is what leads to their profits. The more they lend, the more they make because of the interest rate differential between the deposits they create, and the loans that those deposits fund. As Jackson maintains, this leads to economic instability. He references Taylor (2012) who completed a study that showed that the most reliable predictor of the onset of an economic crisis was past credit growth. As Jackson (2013: 45) quotes Taylor (2012):

> Over 140 years there has been no systematic correlation of financial crises with either prior current account deficits or prior growth in public debt levels. Private credit has always been the only useful and reliable predictive factor.

Governments and central banks have acted in the past to restrict bank activities in money creation that have led to instability and financial crisis. However, in an oft replayed resolution to the question of monetary reform such as this, both the CBI and the Icelandic Financial Services Association (IFSA) were against the proposals put forward to separate the money creation and money lending powers of the banks in Iceland. Primarily their reasoning was that Iceland could not afford to isolate itself financially from the world and the European Union in particular, through the institution of such changes.[116] This was the argument put by Keynes to Fisher back in 1944 (see chapter 3). Essentially one of 'don't rock the boat - the bankers won't like it'.[117] In the end, the Althingi did not vote on the proposal.

6.3.3 Sovereign Money in Switzerland - the Vollgeld-Initiative (VGI)

The Banking school received its greatest scare when Switzerland, as a nation with its own currency and a direct democracy through its system of binding referendums, saw itself as a good candidate for the pursuit of monetary reform. The Swiss peoples' Initiative, which would lead to a binding public referendum, was orchestrated by the NGO the Monetäre Modernisierung (MoMo) (Dawnay 2017). MOMO's aim would be to raise the more than 100,000 signatures required to force the Swiss parliament to hold a Peoples' Initiative the aim of which would be to reform the Swiss monetary system so that: a) the Swiss National Bank would be the sole issuer of money and b) banks would continue to provide all the current services that they do - except they would be prohibited from issuing the medium of exchange. Essentially the VGI is supported by the same arguments made for the NEED Act and the Icelandic Proposal (and the Chicago Plan for that matter). In this instance however, the VGI is put directly to the people to vote upon whereas the NEED Act did not make it to the floor of the House for a vote and the Icelandic inquiry, even though constituted by the Parliament, was not voted upon. What makes the VGI especially interesting is that fact that its passage was not choked at the highest level of government but managed to pass through to the people themselves.

MOMO managed to raise more than 110,000 signatures and these were handed in to the Federal Chancellery in December 2015. The Peoples' Initiative had enough votes to go ahead and eventually in January 2018 the Referendum was set for 10 June 2018. Ironically enough, there were two items on the ballot: one about the banning of online gambling and the other being the sovereign money initiative. The Referendum needed a majority of votes and a majority of cantonments to vote YES to succeed. Both sides of the debate had ample time to address their case directly to the people. MOMO produced an easily digestible document (Dawnay 2017) which sets out the arguments for a monetary transformation to a Sovereign Money Creation system with their arguments being extensively reliant on Huber's vision for Sovereign Money (see 6.2 above). Essentially MOMO had two underlying motivations: firstly, it believed that the split circuit fractional reserve monetary system was the underlying cause of economic volatility and crisis and secondly that Switzerland's system of direct democracy, and the fact that it had its own currency, meant that it was a good candidate for monetary reform (Dawnay 2017: 4). On the other side of the debate, although the conservative financial interests within Switzerland felt sure that like the NEED Act and the Icelandic inquiry the Referendum would fail, nevertheless since it was a broad appeal to the people they marshalled considerable resources in the campaign 'against' the VGI.

The 'pro' and 'against' protagonists for the VGI came together to debate the issue at a conference held on 5 February 2018 and organised by GDI Gottlieb Duttweiler Institute, an independent think tank based in Zurich.[118] The 'YES' case, made by academics such as Joseph Huber, and economists such as Richard Werner and Larry Kotlikoff had the makings of the centuries' old currency school arguments. Essentially, they argued that allowing a private banking system to be the providers of the nation's monetary supply through the creation of debt liabilities, simply focused the country's resources towards the benefit of the owners of that industry. The subsequent side effects of an over-geared financial system leading to economic collapse would have to be sorted out by the government and the public taxpayer. The case for 'NO' was made by the entrenched banking interests represented by the Swiss National Bank and the Federal Council (Swiss Government). Essentially their case was pointed towards a fear of the unknown, a simplistic and altruistic description of the function of banks, as well as a distortion of the Sovereign Money proposal.

The Federal council (Swiss Government) was also strongly

opposed to the proposed Sovereign Money reforms. In their view (Popular initiative 2018) there is no precedent in any developed country in the world for such a monetary system. Furthermore, it would weaken the financial system to the detriment of customers as well as giving the SNB too much power and create the potential for political intervention to increase spending, for example. In the end the initiative failed to gather the votes required to pass. In a press release dated the day of the Referendum, 10 June 2018 (Vollgeld-Initiative 2018), the SMIC stated that 26% had voted for the Initiative. The MOMO accused the Federal Council and the SNB of running a campaign of misinformation and fear. According to MOMO the result was a respectable outcome considering only 38% of the population voted and the resources behind the NO campaign. Many of the NO votes were cast under a distorted view of how banking worked and under the belief of 'better the devil you know'. MOMO have now also brought a legal case against the Federal council for conveying misleading information.

6.4 Postscript: Central Bank Digital Currencies (CBDC)

In his important paper James Tobin (1987) discusses the incidence of Federal Depository Insurance allowing banks to seek higher returns from riskier loans by paying higher interest to short term deposits. Depositors would rely on the depository insurance in the case of a bank failure. The removal of such a risk to the banking system would come about if the government could make available to the public 'a medium with the convenience of deposits and the safety of currency' (Tobin 1987: 172). Tobin could not have anticipated the technology that has evolved since then in the sphere of digital payments, but if he had he would certainly have felt redeemed in his thinking. The Central Bank Digital Currencies (CBDC) proposals discussed below propose to fulfil Tobin's conceptual system of 'cash' functioning not as a commercial bank liability, but as a digital version of the central bank banknote. Through this 'deposited currency' (Tobin 1987: 172) Tobin's desire to remove from society the prospect of a bank failure triggering a run on non-existent cash purporting to support deposits would be achieved.

On 19 April 2021 an announcement was made by the Bank of England and HM Treasury about the establishment of a joint CBDC taskforce to investigate the potential take up of CBDC in the UK (BOE 2021 (a)). As the announcement stated:

> A CBDC would be a new form of digital money issued by the Bank of England and for use by households and businesses. It would exist alongside cash and bank deposits, rather than replacing them.

The statement was explicit about the fact that it had not yet decided whether to take up a CBDC System, although the Bank of England has carried out extensive research in this field. Further research on the introduction of CBDC has been carried out by the Bank for International Settlements (Auer and Boehme 2020), the Reserve Bank of Australia (Richards 2020), Board of Governors of the Federal Reserve (FED BG 2022), Positive Money (Dyson and Hodgson 2016) and Huber (Huber 2019). Positive money and Huber are proponents of Sovereign Money Creation, and it is from that perspective that their contributions to the CBDC discussions evolve. The research from the Central Banks is more from the evolution of payments systems however the connection to Tobin's 'deposited currency' principle discussed above cannot be ignored.

In a speech given by Ben Broadbent, Deputy Governor for Monetary Policy, Bank of England to the London School of Economics on March 2016 (Broadbent 2016), he succinctly itemised the two main points that would be considered by the Bank of England in considering whether to implement a CBDC. As it happens, these are the two central points underpinning the Chicago Plan, 100%

Money and Sovereign Money arguments. Broadbent raised these two issues (Broadbent 2016: 3):

1) the ability for households and businesses to shift retail deposits from commercial banks to the central bank would probably make them safer. Knight, Simons, Fisher, Soddy, Huber, Dyson and many others referred to in this essay would agree with this point. As Broadbent himself explains in the same point commercial bank deposits are backed mainly by illiquid loans that can't be sold easily on the open market. Commercial bank money however does ostensibly have minimal credit and liquidity risk due to federal deposit insurance, tight regulatory supervision and access to central bank liquidity. The decision would be whether, and for what portion of funds, businesses and households determine that central bank digital liabilities (CBDCs) are superior to commercial bank liabilities.

2) secondly, Broadbent suggests that the removal of commercial bank deposits would withdraw the main source of funding for the loans extended. Banks would have to rely on other sources of real funds to support their loan assets. This would only be the case if banks were prohibited from issuing deposits as loans. As Huber (2019: 79) says:

> Under fractional reserve banking, deposits are not loanable funds for the banks, and banks are not financial intermediaries but creators, de- and re-activators and extinguishers of bankmoney.

These are the two points required by the monetary reformists of the 1930s and post GFC 2007/09. For the Bank of England and other central banks however, their main concern seems to be the impact that the shifting of digital deposits from commercial bank issuance to central bank issuance will have on commercial bank funding, its ability to issue credit and the payments system.

The transition from commercial deposit accounts to 'deposited currency', or as Dyson and Hodgson (2016: 1) refer to it, 'digital cash' accounts needs to be managed very carefully. One potential objection to the introduction of CBDC accounts is that their introduction might lead to a run on commercial bank digital deposit accounts (Dyson and Hodgson 2016), simply because as Broadbent mentions above, CBDC accounts offer more safety. Dyson and Hodgson argue such a run would oblige the Bank of England to add reserves to the banking system to accommodate the demand for liquidity. Huber (2019) sees problems in operating commercial and central bank digital accounts in tandem. This relates to his theorising on sovereign money creation. As he wrote (Huber 2017: 64) the fractional reserves system operates as a split (or dual) circuit monetary system. If central bank theorising around the introduction of CBDC accounts does not acknowledge the difficulties in maintaining such as system then the ability of banks to create money through loans will continue, and this is seen as the underlying problem leading to financial instability in the first place (Huber 2019). The sovereign money argument would be to revert to a single circuit monetary system as described in section 6.2 above. This would necessitate, for example as laid out in the American NEED Act 2011 by Representative Kucinich, that on an effective date the conversion of all deposit liabilities held by depository institutions, be designated central bank liabilities digital cash accounts.

President Roosevelt had the opportunity but as has been argued by some, not the courage to mandate 100% full reserve banking during the New Deal Reforms (see 3.4 above). The current extensive and comprehensive discussions by central banks, governments and supranational institutions around CBDC is approaching the issue divide between commercial bank liabilities as money, and central bank liabilities as money, from the efficient payments system point of view. There has been some discussion around the fact that central bank digital cash is a safer proposition to commercial bank digital cash but that does not appear to be the main driver. In effect central banks appear to be 'tiptoeing' around the issue without in fact confronting the elephant in the room head on. That is, that the stability of the medium of exchange is at risk due to private banks increasing or decreasing the money supply through their ability to issue deposits as debt. A recent Bank of England report (BOE 2021 (b)) is diverting from the sovereign money potential of CBDC by discussing the availability of privately managed digital 'stable coins'. So that there may be a money system comprised of various digital coins. As Huber (2019: 87) writes central banks and governments need the courage to make a full transition from bank money to CBDC. Nevertheless, any dilution of the near monopoly that private institutions have, to create the medium of exchange, can only be a good thing.

6.5 Conclusion

The inevitable financial crisis of 2007/09 reinvigorated the arguments put during the Great Depression for monetary reform. Again, the problem as seen by many academics and economists was that banking, through its power to create the medium of exchange had too much of an impact and reach into broader society. Therefore, every time banking and finance as an industry gets into trouble, the government has had to bail it out because of the potential threat to the broader economy. The public, through no fault of its own, and regardless of its general risk adverse nature, has had to make good the debts generated by highly remunerated risk takers in the financial game. In this chapter Joseph Huber from Martin Luther King university in Germany, was relied upon for his Sovereign Money Creation theories. We saw in Section 6.2 how his SMC theory could be applied in practice using a model of the current futures and securities clearing systems. In these two examples, the sovereign issues money as an asset to society. The public transacts using the banks only as agents when it seeks to move funds into and out of consumption. Excess public savings can be invested with commercial banks at risk in return for an expected return. Under an SMC system banks would have only their owners and investors to bail them out in the event of crises through bad or over geared investments.

Section 6.3 briefly looked at three attempts at monetary reform: the NEED Act (USA) 2011/12; the Icelandic Inquiry 2015; the Swiss Peoples' Initiative 2018. All three attempts failed to be enacted. They did however serve to put into the public domain the arguments articulated during the 1930s by the Chicago Plan, Irving fisher and others. Joseph Huber's proposal for a Sovereign Money Creation variant to 100% full reserves banking was favoured by all three reform attempts that were investigated suggesting that the 100% reserves proposals were sub-optimal. James Buchanan, as a pupil of Simons and Knight, was used as a connection between the Old Chicago thinking on the role of the state in guaranteeing a liberal and free economy, and the contemporary view of constitutional money. As all protagonists in these three enquiries would attest, money, the nation's medium of exchange, is such an important part of society that it can only be issued by the people for the people. For this to occur, Joseph Huber detailed how our split circuit money system must revert to a single circuit money system. Banks would only stand between people and their savings as a service provider. Customer money would be protected under money segregation laws which mean that all client money must remain 'off balance sheet' with the banks. The ownership of people's savings is their own. And its repository is with the central bank or some other constitutional entity.

Section 6.4 Central Bank Digital Currency dealt with the current research being carried out investigating the potential issuance of

CBDC by central banks. Tobin (1987) coined the term 'deposited currency' and Dyson and Hodgson (2019: 1) calls it 'digital cash'. CBDC infers the use of modern payments technology to allow household and non-financial business to also be able to access central bank money. This concept would tie in with Huber's call for a single circuit monetary system. Even though earlier research acknowledged the benefit of the safety of CBDC as compared to commercial bank money (Broadbent 2016) more recent research (BOE 2021 (b)) discusses the possibility of central bank regulated digital 'stable coins'. This appears to be an early dilution of central bank resolve to address the instability of the money supply. The argument is made by Huber (2019) that the main issue should remain the possibility of a sovereign money single circuit system. The discussions around CBDC are encouraging but the banking industry (bank school) has if anything grown stronger after every crisis. It has certainly grown larger. Where the impetus for needed monetary reform will come from, as so loudly put by Soddy, Knight, Simons, Fisher, Friedman, Minsky and so many other scholars over the last two hundred years, remains to be seen.

Chapter 7
Conclusion

This book has at its roots the formation of the Federal Reserve System in the U.S.A. in 1913. According to Minsky (1998: 16) the passing of this Act marked the point where the medium of exchange reverted from being 'monetized government debt' to one which was 'monetized private debt'. From there we travelled through the painful years of the 1930s and the Great Depression. We paused in the 1980s to consider the rescue of a substantial banking institution and the failure of regulatory agencies to forecast its collapse. From there we moved to the 2007/09 Great Financial Crisis. Along the way this project has concerned itself with many things, but like strands woven around a single stem, the core theme has been that what is really a public good, the supply of a medium to facilitate the exchange of goods and services amongst the people, has become a coveted private enterprise. This has been a privilege indeed for the banking industry since money has come to the forefront of all utilities as Hicks (1935: 3) wrote: '[p]eople do choose to have money rather than other things, and therefore, in the relevant sense, money must have a marginal utility'. Yet it is the most written about but less understood topic in economics. John Hicks approached the topic 'with peculiar diffidence and even apprehension' (Hicks 1935: 1). Knut Wicksell suggested that 'an approximately complete bibliography (of money) would fill an octavo volume of over 300 pages' (Wicksell 1978: 2). What is it? Is it simply 'the oil in machinery' (Wicksell 1978: 5), facilitating exchange without any causality?

This thesis has, through the history of economic thought, shown that first and foremost money is in the main, a bank created credit. In chapter 2 Frank Vanderlip described in 1908 how money is a bank inter positioning of an individual's liability with the bank's liability.[120] Such is still the case today. Money comes into existence when a bank grants a loan to an individual, thus enhancing the individual's present value spending power in return for their future value income streams. There are two things at play here. Firstly, the demand for the loan and secondly the ability to grant it. Goodhart (2017) told us in chapter 4 that banks are service providers, filling an initial demand by a client. That may be but it is worth bearing in mind that both of these sides to money are motivated by a desire for profit. An entrepreneur wants to borrow capital for a profit-making project and a bank wants to lend capital to earn the interest from it. The more the bank lends the more profit it makes. What better way to secure profits for a bank than to chain all future income streams to present value loans that are in fact created through entries on a balance sheet? This serves to explain the process of financialisation that has occurred from the 1970s.

Today the process of reproduction itself is dependent upon money (Federici, 2014), meaning that all future income streams, including households and not just the profit seeking entrepreneurs, are now captured by the banking system. Professor Seligman describes this process well in the Columbia 1908 conference referred to in chapter 2. If money is a bank created credit, then it can safely be said that money is also a bank created debt. It is a long-term debt to the bank by the client, and it is a short-term debt to the client by the bank. The former is the 'buyer' of the debt, to be paid for with a future income stream. The latter is the 'seller' of the debt, remuneration for which is the interest income stream. When the debt is eventually paid the original loan is 'decreated' and the interest remains. Therefore, any story about money must also concern itself with where money comes from. Frederick Soddy (1933: 84) referred to this as follows:

> As there are shops for dealing in bread, in furniture, in clothes and every other species of property, so there are shops—some of the most palatial structures of modern times—for the express purpose of dealing in Debts; and those shops are called BANKS.'

The logics of the arguments for 100% reserves banking made in chapter 3, or sovereign money made in chapter 6, are attractive. Under the implementation of either monetary reform households and businesses, which are not in the main large financial risk takers, would feel that their savings are not put at credit or liquidity risk through being liabilities of private banking corporations, which are large risk takers. Excesses in the swings and roundabouts in the growth and contraction of the money supply would be curbed thus not artificially impacting on business cycles. All of this would seem possible if banks had their power to issue short term liabilities, which are accepted as the medium of exchange, removed, or even curtailed. In this regard, Turner (2016) makes the point that rather than constantly struggle to fix problems of excessive debt creation by the banks through regulation, attempts at structural reform might be a better solution. As this essay has shown however, this has been elusive. Maybe this is because as Turner continues, that allowing the government to create fiat money in replacement of private bank liability deposits poses its own risks. The banking school will argue that banks are closer to the market for capital and their understanding of funding requirements are superior to that of a centralised committee setting. The ebbs and flows of entrepreneurs' requirements for capital can be capricious and banks, through their ability to provide maturity transformation enable long term investments to be funded with short term liabilities.

The first real challenge to the new banking arrangements post the Federal Reserve Act of 1913 came in the guise of the Chicago Plan in the 1930s. The marker for this inquiry was the episode of the Great Depression. Chapter 3 deals with this economic crisis of the 1930s and the proposals for change that emanated as a consequence. The fact that President Roosevelt failed to take the opportunity to install the full Chicago Plan reforms revolved around two issues. Firstly, as I show in chapter 3, the proponents of the Chicago Plan were not clear, and in fact at odds over how to implement the plan. Henry Simons wanted dramatic change to banking and full reserves for term as well as on demand deposits. Irving Fisher was content to leave banking fairly much alone and only impose full reserves upon on demand deposits. Why they wanted to impose some sort of enhanced regulatory framework around banking however was quite clear: the influence that commercial banks had over the money supply was seen as being an important causal determinant to the business cycle. The second reason for Roosevelt's failure to remove such a profitable privilege from the banking industry may well be attributable to the sway that 'haute finance' had (has) over policy makers. The question of why the banking industry had (has) so much influence over policy makers is an undercurrent running through this essay. Karl Polanyi in his book The Great Transformation (1944), provides a clue as to the power of 'haute finance' to influence governments around the world through the last quarter of the 19th century and the first quarter of the 20th. This '*suis generis*' (Polanyi 1944: 10 - italics in original) organisation of high finance was responsible for the maintenance of peace during the period 1815 to 1914. Independent from governments and institutions such as the Bank of England yet intimately connected with them, groups such as the Rothchilds family:

> embodied the abstract principle of internationalism; their loyalty was to a firm, the credit of which had become the only supranational link between political government and industrial effort in a swiftly growing world economy. (Polanyi 1944: 10)

Already by the end of the 19th century sovereign nations were held on the shoulders of international finance (Polanyi 1944: 14).

The second real challenge to the banking industry ownership of the money supply came after the disaster of the Great Financial Crisis. In chapter 6 we examine Huber's (2015, 2017) and Dyson's (2016) conceptions of sovereign money. Huber describes the current monetary paradigm as being a 'split circuit banking' system. Here there are essentially two types of money. Primary central bank money which is seen as a risk-free repository of wealth, but only accessible to banks and risky secondary money, which is an issue of short-term bank liabilities. The public is not given the option of which type of money it can hold. It can only hold risky bank money. The three sovereign money inquiries discussed in this chapter examine the possibility of converting the split circuit money system into a single circuit money system. The section on Central Bank Digital Currencies suggests such a possibility. CBDCs suggest that households and businesses may choose to hold either central bank money or risky bank money. Although this research is still at an early stage it may provide a pathway for change that has not yet been achievable.

The differences and advantages of a sovereign money system to the Chicago Plan are apparent in that a single circuit monetary system is compelling in its simplicity. We saw in chapter 6 the potential working of such a system as a mirror image of the current workings of the futures and securities systems. Here banks become service providers with only one type of money supply, primary or central bank money. Under strict segregation and client money laws client moneys are at all times off balance sheet for the banks. The Chicago plan by comparison appears complex and unworkable, as shown in chapter 3, specially through Angell's criticism of the Plan. Goodhart (2015: 24) referred to this weakness in the Chicago Plan as its 'Achilles Heel'. It was simply too cumbersome to encompass a 100% reserves system where the banking industry was still able to create short term liabilities that represented spending power in the form of time deposits. The source of spending power, rather than being funnelled and controlled by this intermediating banking industry, is better derived directly from the originating source of wealth in the nation. That is the commons, or the 'commonwealth', or the sovereign. This is what the three inquiries examined. It is the basis of sovereign money creation proposed by Huber and Dyson and many others. Its pedigree goes way back. Abraham Lincoln wrote, shortly before being assassinated:

> The Government should create, issue, and circulate all the currency and credit needed to satisfy the spending power of the Government and the buying power of consumers. The privilege of creating and issuing money is not only the supreme prerogative of Government, but it is the Government's greatest creative opportunity. By adoption of these principles, the long-felt want for a uniform medium will be satisfied. The taxpayers will be saved immense sums of interest, discounts, and exchanges. The financing of all public enterprise, the maintenance of stable government and ordered progress, and the conduct of the Treasury will become matters of practical administration. The people can and will be furnished with a currency as safe as their own Government. Money will cease to be master and become servant of humanity. Democracy will rise superior to the money power. (Abraham Lincoln, 1865, as quoted in Boyle 2015: 95).

Lincoln's idealistic views on the power of the sovereign to issue a stable medium of exchange are not discussed today in orthodox economics. I ask: how could society ever constitute itself so that the medium of exchange that facilitated its reproduction was sourced, not even as monetised government debt as the Chicago Plan proposed, but as freely issued spending power with its base an asset representing an 'nth%' fraction of the total spending power of the nation per unit, as would be the case under a sovereign money system. In any case, certainly not monetised private debt. That concept was abhorrent to Frank Knight and Frederick Soddy and many others. The world has moved on from Lincoln's words, but has it moved so far that we are by necessity completely enmeshed in the banking school view? Mehrling believes that we can learn more from the practitioners in the financial markets. This is true. Those that can do, and those that can't, write about it.[121] It is however Mehrling's 'plumbers who spend their days doing business inside the money markets' (Mehrling 2011: 93), that are the direct innovators and proponents of the financial structures that lead to financial overdrive and crisis. They have been positioning themselves as the oracles of reason on how society can best constitute itself since Fisher's goldsmiths of the 15th century. What do Lincoln's words say about the character required by the politician that will agitate for the monetary reform sought by the proponents of the Chicago plan and sovereign money? Can the currency school ever regain the ascendancy in this perpetual debate against the banking school?

There are many, many authors on whose shoulders this story stands and a giant amongst them was Hyman Minsky, who had studied under Simons and Schumpeter. He wrote early and at length about what stands at the core of this story. Financial volatility, he wrote often, was a cause of the fact that the money supply is endogenous to the banking system. As he wrote (Minsky 1964: 324) 'the evidence that money is a significant part of the mechanism generating a deep depression is strong '. There are echoes of fisher's (1933) debt deflation theory here. The economy can 'chug' along nicely enjoying an expansionary phase. During this period all seems fine and gradually as confidence in the future growth continues to build so does leverage. Writing in 1964 Minsky was already questioning whether another 'deep depression' (Minsky 1964: 325) might occur since banking and finance had changed to such an extent. This steady expansionary phase triggers changes in the structure of the financial sector. In my words the jug is gradually filling with water until it overflows. The jug being the economy, and the water being confidence which is morphing into hubris. It is the unmaking of many a great trader, and it is a human instinct.

Minsky's taxonomy of the evolution of a financial system from hedge, to speculative to ponzi comes to mind. Minsky was a proponent of the 100% reserve banking methodology for the issuance of the money supply. He details his view comprehensively on this as recently as in 1994, a couple of years before his death (Minsky 1998). He certainly was not a 'plumber' but rather a 'teacher'. So, his writings about the evolution of finance from a stable mode to one of instability were not listened to. Minsky wrote in this same paper that 'every economic policy argument reflects a maintained economic theory' (Minsky 1998: 3). Very true but what do economists theorise about? Where is the bedrock for an argument about how we constitute ourselves as humans in a fair and equitable, as well as sustainable society.

To this end, Soddy's insistence on anchoring economics to the physical laws of thermodynamics (Soddy 1922, 1933) have substance. They are appealing because there is nowhere else to go. The natural way of things cannot be managed by man. Although they strive to do so. I leave the very last words to Soddy then, because it was his words that got me started on this project in the first place.

> 'We cannot progress a step in this subject unless we can devise a monetary system in which the money is issued neither for

usury nor in response to political pressure from this or that particular interest, but by the nation solely and freely as it is required to keep its value in relation to wealth as constant as is possible from century to century. Any ideal short of this is simply to accept Stephen Leacock's[122] definition of political economy as that which teaches we know nothing of the laws of wealth.' (Soddy 1933: 155)

Notes

1 Introduction pp. 13-19

[1] Schumpeter (1939: 152) has something to say about Fisher's writings on too much debt. He suggests that the only way to define over indebtedness is via benchmarking to productivity. An increase in debt without a commensurate increase in productivity would lead 'to a fall in prices, sometimes leading to disaster'. Goodhart (2017: 48) writes that the Banking School dictum of old was that if banks followed the real bills doctrine that lending would be in tune with production and the lending for speculative purposes was to be frowned upon. He relates this to the exchange equation MV = PY so that if money (M) rises in proportion to real output (Y) then prices (P) would remain constant.

2 Credit Creation Banking pp. 20-31

[2] Schumpeter (1954: 303) writes regarding bank credit and money: 'The clear perception of the truth that a bank note and a checking deposit are fundamentally the same thing is in fact one of the strong points of this theory. Thus money remains very strictly defined. Credit, particularly bank credit, is merely a method of using it more efficiently.' Furthermore, if bank credit is seen as a 'claim' to money he reasons: 'The only answer to the question why this is so is that there is no other case in which a claim to a thing can, within limits to be sure, serve the same purpose as the thing itself: you cannot ride on a claim to a horse, but you can pay with a claim to money. But this is a strong reason for calling money what purports to be a claim to legal money, provided it does serve as means of

payment.' (1986: 305). I am very grateful to Schumpeter for leading me to Charles Rist's *History of Money and Credit Theory*, in his footnote 3 p 304.

[3] Other financial institutions have the capacity to issue credit but unlike banks, those liabilities are not exchangeable for central bank money.

[4] Bezemer (2016: 1275) writes that the accounting convention in commerce has existed since prehistoric times. Accounting was necessary to record the hierarchies of moneys 'which structure the growth and volume of credit and debt, and the range of its permissible uses. These accounting relations have been central in organizing production and exchange'.

[6] The First Bank of the United States was chartered in 1791 and had its charter expire in 1811; the Second Bank of the United States was chartered in 1816 and its charter expired in 1836 after heavy lobbying by President Andrew Jackson. See Johnson 2010 for a good summary of these events.

[7] According to Johnson & Kwak, (2010: 26) the origins of the 1907 crisis can be put down to an attempt to manipulate the stock price of the United Copper Company by insiders and their bankers. The plan went awry causing a run on banks connected to the scheme. Forced to raise cash quickly banks sold assets at firesale prices putting downward pressure on stocks. Banks cut back loans to stockbrokers putting further pressure on prices across the board. This was symptomatic of past and future crises to come. It highlighted the Achilles Heel of fractional reserves banking - having floating liabilities matched with fixed assets. It also highlighted the real need for a Central Bank to provide required reserves in such situations.

[8] Johnson 2010 describes how imposition of a 10% tax on banknotes issued by state-chartered banks under the American National Banking Act of 1863, 64 and 65 led them to rely on chequing deposits instead. He says on page 13: 'To the surprise of many who had supported the national banking legislation, state-chartered banks were able to survive even though they no longer had the incentive to issue bank notes mainly because the use of checks was increasing rapidly. As a result, demand

deposits (checking accounts) and not bank note issues became the most important source of funds to the banks.'

Phillips 2014: 243 also writes about this: 'In the United States, this practice became less frequent, at least at the state level, when Congress placed a punitive tax on state-chartered banks' notes during the Civil War to increase demand for the Treasury's Greenbacks. Adapting to this restriction, banks turned their efforts to checkable demand deposit accounts (checking accounts) as a means of keeping the game (or "money multiplying") going.'

For a description of the greater usage of chequing accounts in the United Kingdom after the 1844 Peel act see Hollis, C. 1937, *The Breakdown of Money: An Historical Explanation.* It seems that like the British, the Americans did not see checking deposits as a replacement for banknotes.

[9] Also, Davies (2002) gives a historical accounting for the development of the Currency/Banking school controversies which evolved from the bullionist/anti-bullionist arguments in the early 19th century.

[10] In a submission to the Democratic Caucus as it was debating the Owen-Glass bill, Paul Warburg made his feeling known regarding the ownership and control of any central bank. as he said: 'The strong argument in favor of this theory is that central banking, like any other banking, is based on "sound credit," that the judging of credits is a matter of business which should be left in the hands of businessmen, and that the Government should be kept out of business.'(Warburg 1913).

[11] The Marxist academic Nikitin (1983: 155) could not disagree more with Seligman's neoclassical depiction of the crises of capitalism. Nikitin writes: 'But the striving to expand production endlessly is not backed up by a corresponding expansion of consumption. Moreover, the striving to receive maximum profit induces capitalists to reduce wages and step up the degree of exploitation. But increased exploitation and impoverishment of the working people means a relative drop in effective demand and diminishes opportunities for selling commodities. The result of all this is economic crises of overproduction.'

[12] As we will soon see, Irving Fisher had a different view - putting the

contraction of the Great Depression down to a 30% reduction in the money supply by banks.

[13] Wicksell (1978: 5) describes it as 'the oil in machinery'.

[14] Another contribution to the Columbia conference was made by Paul Warburg. There is not enough room here to deal with his important essay but as Bordo & Wheelock 2010 (10) write: Warburg convinced Nelson Aldrich, Chairman of the Senate Committee on Banking and Currency 'that recreating as closely as possible the money market environment of England, France and Germany was a crucial step in bringing stability to the U.S. banking system'. The internationalisation of the movement of credit would be complete, and the capstone finally set in place, with the creation of the FED.

[15] See: https://www.federalreservehistory.org/people/frank_arthur_vanderlip

[16] See: Wray, L.R. 1993, for more on the development of the formalist versus the substantive economies. The formalist methodology of the early banking cartels bumped into the strong institutionalist substantive criticism of the 1930s as a consequence of the Great Depression. There are purposeful echoes here of Polanyi's 'double Movement'.

[17] Vanderlip pre-empts what Minsky said about this in his 1986 *Stabilising an Unstable Economy*, p. 256: 'Banking is not money lending; to lend, a money lender must have money. The fundamental banking activity is accepting, that is, guaranteeing that some party is creditworthy. A bank, by accepting a debt instrument, agrees to make specified payments if the debtor will not or cannot. Such an accepted or endorsed note can then be sold in the open market. A bank loan is equivalent to a bank's buying a note that it has accepted.'

Minsky was simply describing what Vanderlip, and the other bankers were already doing 100 years earlier.

See also Werner 2016: 367 where he quotes Howe 1915: 15 on the assertion that 95% of all payments are made by bank cheque and thus corroborating Vanderlip.

[18] In Hart&Mehrling (1995: 6) Albert Hart describes this process well: 'When banks create money by making loans, they grant to borrowers

the power to make purchases. The ability of borrowers to obtain goods in exchange for their own IOUs is generally limited by the willingness of their suppliers to extend trade credit. However, once their IOUs have been accepted by a bank, so that the bank guarantees payment, they become widely acceptable.'

[19] As Ingham (2004: 18) wrote: 'orthodox mainstream economic theory, as this developed from the late nineteenth century, concluded that money itself was not analytically significant. The fundamental meta-theory is expressed in the model of a 'real' economy comprising myriad bilateral exchanges between rational maximizing agents. Money is seen as a 'neutral veil' over these essentially barter exchanges '.

[20] Schumpeter (1954: 1080) discusses this at length. In footnote 5 he addresses Keynes' view on this and questions why Keynes regressed in his General Theory (1936) to an old view that savings leads to investments. He had in fact in his Treatise (1930) steered towards Schumpeter's view that bank loans create deposits. In other words, investments lead to savings. Chick (1992: 201) disagrees with Schumpeter: 'In Keynesian theory, investment evoked saving through income-creation: the initiative came from entrepreneurs and depended on their expectation of long-run profit potential'. Keynes (1936) quite clearly interprets savings as coming from investments as he wrote (1936: 64) "Saving, in fact, is a mere residual. The decisions to consume and the decisions to invest between them determine incomes. Assuming that the decisions to invest become effective, they must in doing so either curtail consumption or expand income. Thus the act of investment in itself cannot help causing the residual or margin, which we call saving, to increase by a corresponding amount.'

We will discuss further in Ch 6 that as Fuller (2018) writes it is only under a 100% reserves (or a sovereign money) system where loans can emanate from savings. Chick (1992: 195) under her stage 1 of banking model also suggests that early banking operated based on savings predominantly fostering investments before fractional reserves banking became commonplace. Under credit creation banking however there are greater sums of media of circulation created through the issuance of loans to deposits than there are available savings. Therefore, investments will lead to savings.

[21] Minsky (1998: 16) describes that what the bankers were really after was to substitute a currency which was in effect monetised government debt with a currency that was monetised private debt.

[22] As Karl Polanyi wrote in 1944 (The Great Transformation 1957: 225), the chartering of the independent Bank of England marked the separation of the state from business - '[c]ommercial capital had won its tilt against the Crown.' This may have been the beginning of the banking school's campaign to win control of the issuance of the medium of exchange.

Frederick Soddy also has something to say about the formation of the Bank of England: 'Reverting to the transition from the old to the new system, before banking started there was a definite amount of gold and silver coinage only. The first step on the downward path, from money for use to money for usury, was the power conferred upon the Bank of England to issue banknotes to a limited extent in return for the loan of money to the Government…' (Wealth 1933: 140)

[23] See for example: Bezemer, D.J. 2016; Goodhart, C.A., Jensen, M.A. & others 2015; Werner, R.A. 2014; Werner, RA 2016; Jakab, Z. & Kumhof, M. 2019; Beneš, J. & Kumhof, M. 2012.

3 First Debate on Monetary Reform pp. 32-70

[24] This group included Garfield Cox, Aaron Director, Paul Douglas, Frank Knight, Albert G. Hart, Lloyd Mints, Henry Schultz, and Henry Simons.

[25] According to Demeulemeester (2018: n2) the term "Chicago Plan" was coined by Hart (1935), whereas "100% money" was Fisher's phrasing.

[26] Leeson's (ed.) *Keynes, Chicago, and Friedman, Vols 1 and 2* comprehensively covers the evolution of the 'oral tradition' of the quantity theory by academics at the 'Chicago School'. Leeson describes in the introduction the claim by Friedman that in his *Studies in the Quantity Theory of Money* (1956) 'he was merely formalising the macroeconomic ideas of the first generation of Chicago School at whose "feet he sat" in 1932-3

and 1934-5. This essay does not deal with this aspect of the Chicago School tradition, but it is important to have a sense for the thinking of Simons and Knight, two of the participants (to whom Friedman credits the origination of this tradition) with whom we do deal here.

[27] As Soddy says in Wealth (1933: 140): 'The whole intentions of the latter Act, which is still the law—namely, to prevent the issue of paper money uncovered by gold—were frustrated by the development of the cheque system. The latter effectively killed the bank-note as a form of currency by establishing a much more insidious and uncontrollable form.'

Phillips (1995: 90) writes that Simons was preoccupied with the way that banks 'dodged' the British Act of 1844. The Act was Simons' motivation for his reform proposals, and he was adamant that it encompassed all possible means of payments, not just on demand deposits.

[28] See: Mises, L. von 1912, *The Theory of Money and Credit* from p.399 for the Austrian view on this. Mises adds much to the argument that the Banking Act of 1844 should have broadened its scope to include fiduciary media as well as banknotes.

[29] The Base 1000 Index is a common measure used by the funds management industry to track and compare the growth in different assets over time. Comparing absolute values would not provide a meaningful indication of the relevant growth/decline in these varied financial indicators. A value of 1000 is allocated to each indicator as at December 1914. The respective rates of annual growth are then applied to each indicator using the formula b x (1 + n%) where b = last close of the index (start reading is 1000) and n% = the annual rate of return for that indicator.

[30] For purposes of this essay annual figures are taken so actual peaks and troughs are not captured - however the major trends are. For example, the stock market in the United States, as measured by the Dow Jones Index, peaked 3 September 1929 at 381.17 for a total gain from December 1914 of 598%. The subsequent decline took it down to a low of 42.68 on 7 December 1932 for a total decline of 89%!

[31] A drawdown chart shows the peak to valley drop in an investment or asset class. Generally shown as a % drop it helps in visualising relative volatilities, and it is extensively used in the funds management industry

to assess potential investments. Drawdowns are important in assessing declines in value from a previous high - shown as the 0% line - in monetary terms as well as in determining the time that it takes an asset to recover losses and make a new high. The drawdown chart emphasises the deflationary periods of negative growth.

[32] The risk assets to capital relationship is referred to as the Solvency Ratio. The deposits to reserves relationship is referred to as the Liquidity Ratio. These two bank balance sheet indicators are important to this discussion and are covered in detail in Chapter 4.

[33] Minsky (1998: 9) suggests that the Dow Jones Index fell far more than CPI or wages because 'capital incomes (current, recent and expected) had fallen and only secondarily because the discount factor had risen'. I suspect that another major reason was that the market was so heavily overbought, especially using margin. These overbought positions caved in on themselves and started the slide where the further the price fell the more had to be sold.

[34] The Board of Governors (BG) of the Federal Reserve System (FED) data begins in 1914 - which was the first operational year for the newly constituted body. It also makes sense to mark 1914 as the start of the 'new system of financial organisation' since with the creation of the FED came the creation of a new era for banking.

[35] In an echo of Fisher's Debt Deflation Theory, Minsky wrote in his Financial Instability Hypothesis about markets where momentum grows as the market swings from hedge, to speculative to ponzi in nature (Minsky 1992).

[36] A. G. Hart writes about this in his preface to the book he coauthored with Mehrling *Debt Crisis and Recovery: The 1930s and the 1990s* (1995). Hart, who was an original signatory to the Chicago Plan Memorandum in March 1933, believed that economic processes emanated from institutions and that the role of economists was to understand how these institutions worked.

[37] Soddy first spoke about money in two lectures given November 10 and 17 1921. These lectures were published as 'Cartesian Economics'. He then wrote a further three books (Wealth, Virtual Wealth and Debt 1926,

Money Versus Man 1931 and The Role of Money 1934) on the subject.

[38] Currie from Harvard agreed when he wrote (1938: 358): 'In our system, the ebb and flow of deposits from one bank unit to another entails the necessity, at times other than when large excess reserves are widely diffused, of corresponding shifts in earning assets.'

[39] Bordo & Wheelock (2010: 21) draw on Friedman and Schwartz (1963) when they 'contend that the decline in the money stock was the main cause of the subsequent decline in economic activity'.

[40] See Anderson et al., 2016, Fishback 2010, Bordo & Wheelock 2010 for insights into what the FED did and did not do to stave off the Great Depression.

[41] This is a big story on its own and it could easily swamp the story here, so it is left up to the reader to pursue. It is an important part of the banking school argument however for its continued support for bank issued debt as currency.

[42] According to Fuller (2019), 100% *Banking and Its Advocates: A Brief History*, this was not such a radical proposal at all. In fact, 100%RB banking had been the norm far longer than fractional reserve banking. See: https://mises.org/profile/edward-w-fuller for this informative and comprehensive historical take on 100%RB and its evolution into FRB.

[43] Fisher's Currency Commission is the equivalent of the Chicago Plan's Federal Reserve Banks, whose Federal Reserve Notes would be the equivalent 100% backing for commercial bank on demand deposits.

[44] In a letter from Irving Fisher (1936) to President F.D. Roosevelt Fisher states: '"the chief direct cause of the depression was the one-third reduction of the money stock between 1929 and 1933, and the only sure and rapid recovery was through monetary means."' Quoted from Akin and Dolgun (2016: 95).

[45] Money supply is taken as being Total Deposits + Liquid Assets. As defined by the FED BG: 'The supply of money, in the sense of a means of payment, is generally defined to include currency and demand deposits of banks.'

(Banking and Monetary Statistics 1914-1941 Part I p11)

[46] See note … in 3.1 Introduction above.

[47] The Chicago Plan also proposed that the Federal Reserve Banks guarantee all member bank deposits to arrest the run on bank deposits. The quid pro quo for this being that member banks' affairs were to be managed by the Reserve Banks. Further the Chicago economists were concerned with the stability of money and wanted the price level raised by 15 per cent and held there through currency and fiscal measures. All these measures are dealt at great length by Yeager 1962, Phillips (95), Leeson 2003, and many others and have especially been revived since the onset of the Great Financial Crisis of 2007/08.

[48] There are further useful critiques of 100%RB posed by: Dow, S., Johnsen, G. & Montagnoli, A. 2015, *A critique of full reserve banking*; Goodhart et al., 2015 provides a critique from the banking /currency school perspective; Van Dixhoorn, C. 2013, 'Full Reserve Banking'.

[49] A Positive Program for Laissez Faire: Some Proposals for a Liberal Economic Policy - which is part II of Economic Policy for a Free Society (1948)

[50] George Tavlas, in his timely 2020 paper '*On the Controversy Over the Origins of the Chicago Plan*' details this convincingly. Tavlas dispels the view that the 100% reserves idea, so strongly lobbied for in the Chicago Plan, originated with Frederick Soddy and investigates why Soddy was not cited in the Chicago Plan memoranda.

[51] The other contributors to this discussion piece were Irving Fisher, Wesley C. Mitchell, Melchior Palyi, Waldo F. Mitchell and Karl. G. Karsten. Knight's contribution was by far the shortest.

[52] 'Alleged service' according to Knight (Fisher et al. 1927: 121).

[53] Soddy's book was also reviewed in Dec 1927 by James Angell from Columbia (Angell J.W. 1927). Describing Soddy as 'one of the most distinguished living British scientists' Angell captured what Soddy attempted to do with his book *Wealth, Virtual Wealth and Debt* (1926) when he wrote that it was an attempt to 'to apply certain basic concepts of physics to the complex and shifting phenomena of economic life.' (Angell 1927: 621).

[54] Also see Daly, H.E. 1980, 'The economic thought of Frederick Soddy', and for the only authorised biography of Soddy see Merricks, L. 1996, The world made new...'

[55] When Knight reviewed Soddy's book (Knight 1927) he quickly dismissed one important part of Soddy's argument: 'His effort to establish a conception of physical wealth, subject to a principle of conservation and interpretable in relation to physical energy, must be briefly dismissed. (Knight 1927: 732)'. This part of Soddy's argument in relation to money does not concern us here but it must be noted that as Daly (1986: 487) says, that in consigning Soddy simply as a physical reductionist, Knight neglects an important part of Soddy's theorising about money. According to Daly (1986: 483) 'Soddy anticipated the basic insights of Georgescu-Roegen and Boulding regarding the relation of economics and thermodynamics'. Further, as Daly writes, Soddy argued that '[t]he absurdity of infinite growth has been the most carefully ignored anomaly in the paradigm of modern economics' (Daly 1986: 485).

[56] See Phillips 1995: 47 where he writes about Knight's support of Soddy: 'Hence Frank Knight, acknowledged as one of the greatest economic minds of the twentieth century, embraced the heretical proposal of a non-economist to transform radically the banking system. The growing bank failures of the early thirties, and the eagerness of economists to make policy proposals in a time of crisis, provided Knight and others at Chicago with the opportunity to restate and refine the Soddy proposal'.

[57] Which is a repudiation of the current monetary policy doctrine.

[58] See: Batchelder, R.W. & Glasner, D. 1991, for an interesting discussion on how the appearance of The General Theory swamped pre-Keynesian monetary theories.

[59] Van Horn & Emmett, 2015 write how Knight's interest became more entrenched in the pursuit of ethics in economics and why the liberal ethos was failing. As they say: 'Knight may have taught the Chicago economists price theory, but his emphasis on democratic discussion and ethics diminished his importance to the emerging Chicago approach' (2015: 1444)

[60] This term was borrowed from Askari, H. & Krichene, N. 2016,

'100 Percent Reserve Banking and the Path to a Single-Country Gold Standard' p. 29. They used it in the same context as Knight.

[61] Goodhart et al., 2015: 23 on deals with this extensively. He describes this issue as 'the Achilles heel of the Currency School, and most proponents deal with it by ignoring it.'

[62] Fisher also deals with this in *The Rate of Interest* (1907) chapter V. On page 84 Fisher discusses the difference between the rate of interest on money and the rate of interest on goods. The former he calls 'nominal' and the latter 'real'. The servant in our story will be disadvantaged according to Fisher because when prices are rising, the rate of interest will be high - but not high enough to compensate for the rise in the price of goods. Conversely when prices are falling, the rate of interest will be low but not low enough to compensate for the fall in prices.

63 Fisher was not the only great thinker to go bankrupt through trading the markets. As Richard Swedberg writes in the Introduction to *Capitalism, Socialism and Democracy* (Schumpeter 2003 (1943)), Schumpeter lost everything in 1924 whilst working for the Biedermann Bank. He was later fired from that institution due to a "dubious reputation acquired in the business world".

[64] See: Schumpeter, J.A. 1939: 152. Here Schumpeter discusses Fisher's view on indebtedness. Schumpeter decides that benchmarking debt to GDP might be a good way to measure over-indebtedness:

'Professor Fisher, therefore, rightly emphasizes over indebtedness induced, primarily, by easy money. But he does not define over-indebtedness. Nor is it easy to do so. The only way which the writer can think of is precisely by reference to "productivity." Schumpeter continues that unproductive debt may eventually lead to 'a fall in prices, sometimes leading to disaster…'

[65] This reasoning is further amplified by Minsky's (1992) financial instability hypothesis. In his paper Minsky details the progression through hedge markets to speculative and then finally ponzi markets. In an echo of Fisher's debt deflation theory Minsky writes that the financial instability hypothesis is 'a theory of the impact of debt on system behavior and also incorporates the manner in which debt is validated.' Minsky's

arrow hits the bullseye of what Fisher was preoccupied with, since we inhabit a capitalist system where debt is forever prevalent.

In a more recent study, Jorda et al. (2014: 4) find that credit (debt) is 'particularly influential in shaping business cycle dynamics.' and that 'Recessions that follow larger credit booms tend to be significantly worse, all else equal.' All in support of Fisher's debt deflation theory.

[66] Soddy (1933: 84) describes Credit (debt) as 'the most gigantic species of Property in this country, and the trade in Debts is beyond all comparison the most colossal branch of commerce'.

Smithin, J. 2013, 2016, deals with this effectively. He writes that new money needs to enter the economy continuously to provide the profits of previous borrowers.

Bezemer 2016: 1276 approaches it from the accounting point of view. For him, money is created out of nothing through credit.

[67] This helps to understand current central bank urgency in maintaining interest rates at zero (or even negative in some instances) and the addition of trillions in liquidity, to dissuade hoarding and encourage borrowing. See for example Fishback 2010.

[68] See Keynes 1936: 94 (5) Changes in Fiscal Policy and also 1936: 98 where Keynes writes: 'On the other hand, a decline in income due to a decline in the level of employment, if it goes far, may even cause consumption to exceed income not only by some individuals and institutions using up the financial reserves which they have accumulated in better times, but also by the government, which will be liable, willingly or unwillingly, to run into a budgetary deficit or will provide unemployment relief; for example, out of borrowed money'

[69] In Douglas et al. 1939: 27 the authors write, following Fisher's 100% Money plan: 'Under the present fractional reserve system, the only way to provide the nation with circulating medium for its growing needs is to add continually to our Government's huge bonded debt. Under the 100% reserve system the needed increase in circulating medium can be accomplished without increasing the interest bearing debt of the Government.' It seems under fractional reserve banking, that the government is the final arbiter through its borrowing to add to the money supply.

However, under 100% Money that would not be the case since money would be issued directly by the government, instead of the government 'borrowing' money into existence.

[70] Although there were implementation differences as already mentioned, between the proponents of monetary reform there was universal agreement as to the merits of divorcing money creation and destruction from lending. For example, in Douglas et al. (1939: 2) over 250 academics from 157 universities signalled their approval of such monetary reforms.

[71] On January 24, 1933, Ferdinand Pecora ('the Hellhound of Wall Street') was appointed by the Senate Committee on Banking and Currency as lead council for this Inquiry. The terms of the Inquiry were further broadened on April 4, 1933, and June 8, 1933, to encompass the entire industry of banking and securities dealing. His investigations led to the grilling in the senate of the heads of the major banking firms at the time. Subsequently large penalties were imposed for various fraudulent activities. See: Stock Exchange Practices 1934 (U.S. Government Printing Office).

[72] See Phillips 1992 and Papadimitriou 1996 for in-depth description of the various acts passed during the 1st and 2nd New Deals.

[73] Paradoxically not only did Roosevelt not impose a 100% reserves requirement on the banks but the creation of Federal Deposit insurance in 1935 led to 'a delegation to private enterprises of the government's sovereign right to coin money. The government promises to coin money to meet the depository's promises to its creditors in case it is unable to redeem them itself.' (Tobin 1987: 170).

4 Determination of the Money Supply pp. 71-101

[74] by being the numerators of the liquidity and solvency ratios respectively.

[75] Victoria Chick (1992: 193) wrote that: 'In Chick (1983, ch. 9) it was argued that the reversal of causality in the saving-investment nexus proposed by Keynes (1936) should not be seen as correct theory in triumph over error but as a change in what constituted correct theory

due to the development of the banking system.' The concept that investments lead to savings in fact predates the timing proposed by Chick. It was clearly the case much earlier as proposed by Vanderlip (1908).

[76] See also Sheard, P. 2013, 'Repeat After Me: Banks Cannot And Do Not" Lend Out" Reserves', *Standard & Poors Ratings Direct.*

[77] Chick (1992: 200) would say that this example of monetary expansion is approaching a 'pure credit economy' where money created by the banks never leaves the banking system. It circulates from bank to bank via bank reserve accounts with the central bank until it is repaid to the lending institution.

[78] See: FED Chicago 1994, *Modern Money Mechanics: A Workbook on Bank Reserves and Deposit Expansion*, Federal Reserve Bank of Chicago, Chicago, Ill. p.6 onwards for a comprehensive description of how deposit expansion works.

[79] Mehrling (2011: 93) tangentially touches on this point when he writes that academics and economists need to write about what the practitioners within the banking and financial industry actually do: 'Those who inhabit the world of academic economics and finance have the luxury to abstract from the plumbing behind the walls, but the plumbers who spend their days doing business inside the money markets, behind the walls, do not. It is the plumbers' worldview we must tap if we are to learn the lessons of the current crisis and to build a more robust system going forward.'

[80] It may also be the case that a new borrowing is in the form of an overdraft facility. In such a case the deposit is not created until the facility is drawn down. See Goodhart (2017: 44) and Mehrling (2011: 94) for more on this.

[81] Ravn (2021: 150) goes as far as to say: 'Banks connected in a clearing system have foregone reliance on their own reserves and embraced the powers of netting and clearing, placing their eggs in that collective and much more efficient basket.'

[82] See: https://positivemoney.org/2012/07/if-banks-can-create-money-how-come-northern-rock-went-bust/

Here Positive Money details how a major British Bank, Northern Rock, went bust due to its lending practices being far greater than the market's. Also, as Mehrling (2011: 94) writes: 'Payments elasticity in our decentralized payments system thus depends on interbank credit to relax the "reserve constraint" facing individual banks'. The normal functioning of the banking system no longer relies on individual banks having the required reserves with the central bank to meet payment requirements. Rather it depends on the inter-bank money market where these reserves can be borrowed.

[83] Mehrling et al. 2013 have a lot to say about the systemic need for liquidity by the banking system. On page 12 they note that 'financial crisis is entirely a matter of liquidity and not at all a matter of solvency'. Also, in Mehrling 2011 page 107 the discussion regarding the central bank morphing during a crisis from a 'lender' to a 'dealer' of last resort illuminates the transition in banking from reliance on central bank reserves to a market-based funding system. I deal with this in more detail in chapters 5 and 6.

[84] Non-Bank Financial Institutions have been at the forefront of the development in creative financing especially from the 1980s onwards. Otherwise known as shadow banking, NBFIs were instrumental in the development of the lending products that led to the GFC. These financing organisations operated legally but mainly under the radar of the regulatory institutions, and they are dealt with in detail by Perry Mehrling 2011, 2013. We deal with them in more detail in Chapter 5.

[85] We deal with the development and importance of the shadow banking industry in chapter 5.

[86] See note 9 chapter 2 re the 1907 crash. What was then is also now.

5 Can it Happen Again? pp. 102-129

[87] See: Bernanke (2010) for his rationale for adding liquidity. He writes: 'Lower corporate bond rates will encourage investment. And higher stock prices will boost consumer wealth and help increase confidence, which can also spur spending. Increased spending will lead to higher incomes

and profits that, in a virtuous circle, will further support economic expansion.' The irony lies in the fact that Bernanke felt that by keeping the bubble that had caused the problem in the first place inflated, we might be able to kick the problem down the road.

Valencia et al. (2008: 4) differ with Bernanke. As they write bailing out the financial sector is very costly to the public purse and may lead to 'distortions' that worsen capital allocation decisions once the crisis is resolved.

[88] See Footnote in section 3.2.3 above where Schumpeter discusses Fisher's over indebtedness and surmises that a proper measure for the growth in debt is the comparable growth in productivity through the GDP. Benes and Kumhof (2012: 4) support Fisher's and other more recent empirical work showing that high debt levels, such as those shown before the great Depression and the GFC are predictors of real and financial crises.

[89] See Footnote to figure 3.2.3 above for an explanation of the calculation method used to derive the Base 1000 index relative performances.

[90] Commercial Bank balance sheet data has been collated from Dec 1914 to present time as follows: BG FED 1943, Banking and Monetary Statistics 1914-1941:

Table 18 - ALL MEMBER BANKS PRINCIPAL ASSETS AND LIABILITIES - ON CALL DATES - 1914-1941 (p 72)

BG FED 1976, Banking and Monetary Statistics 1941-1970:

ON CALL DATES - 1942-1970 (p 60)

31/12/1971 Series Break due to change from Member Banks to all domestically chartered commercial Banks

From Dec 1971 - Dec 1973: Annual Statistical Digest 1971-1975 p 64

From Dec 1974 to Current:

H.8 Assets and Liabilities of Domestically Chartered Commercial Banks in the United States

https://www.federalreserve.gov/datadownload/Choose.aspx?rel=H8

[91] Debt numbers used are from the St Louis FED TCMDO series. This series is derived from the FED Flow of Funds Data found at: https://

www.federalreserve.gov/apps/fof/FOFTables.aspx. It is comprised of the following tabulations:
L.208 Debt Securities
L.209 Open Market Paper
L.210 Treasury Securities
L.211 Agency- and GSE-Backed Securities
L.212 Municipal Securities
L.213 Corporate and Foreign Bonds
L.214 Loans
L.215 Depository Institution Loans Not Elsewhere Classified
L.216 Other Loans and Advances
L.217 Total Mortgages
L.218 Home Mortgages
L.219 Multifamily Residential Mortgages
L.220 Commercial Mortgages
L.221 Farm Mortgages
L.222 Consumer Credit
This DEBT data represents the total credit issued to consumers, corporations, and the government within the United States and excludes credit of Financial Corporations.

[92] Geoffrey Ingham (2008: 152) relates Keynes' argument in relation to capital markets. This argument maintains that capital markets have an inherent tendency to become 'unproductive casinos'. In this scenario capital is diverted from productive industrial purposes towards 'bubbles' enhanced through price volatility.

[93] I think that Minsky agrees with the comment that capitalism has directional momentum as he wrote: '[t]he focus is on an accumulating capitalist economy that moves through real calendar time' (Minsky 1992: 2).

[94] As the Alford Cross technique discussed in chapter 4 would suggest, the purchase of $4.5 billion in bad loans by the FDIC would be reflected in CINB's balance sheet as a reduction in risk assets and an increase in cash assets. This translates into an improvement in both the liquidity ratios (cash increases as a % of deposit liabilities) and the solvency ratios (risk assets are reduced compared to equity) of the bank, which is

precisely what it needed.

[95] See note to Figure 3.2.2 above.

[96] James Tobin was not alone when he wrote (1987: 168) 'the ability to shift risk to the federal government is bound to tempt depositors and managers to take more risk' (in reference to the bailout of Continental Illinois Bank in the 1980s).

[97] CINB in fact had to write off $326 million in deposits it had with Penn Square Bank.

[98] Regulation Q was passed by Congress and allowed the Federal Reserve to cap the interest rates that banks and thrifts could pay depositors. Its aim was to stop competitive pressures from increasing bank leverage. Also see Mehrling (2011) for more on Regulation Q.

6 Second Debate on Monetary Reform. Pp. 130-163

[99] See More on this in FED BG 2022: 5, where they discuss that increasingly there is a third type of money which can be referred to as non-bank money. It is not discussed here because this type of money does not have access to federal deposit insurance guarantees nor central bank liquidity and is not a generally acceptable means of payment nor unit of account.

[100] See: Jackson 2013 and Dyson et al. 2016 for comprehensive introductions to sovereign Money Creation.

[101] Except for an overdraft. In this instance, the deposit is created simultaneously with the loan however the deposit is created in the bank account of the payee, not the bank holding the loan asset.

[102] For example, Fisher's 'Currency Commission' discussed in section 3.2 above.

[103] See Angell's criticism of Fisher's plan in section 3.2 above. There Angell suggests that Fisher had vastly overestimated the amount of government bonds held by the banks and that therefore the Currency Commission would have to purchase other bank assets to cover total deposits.

[104] www.positivemoney.org

[105] see: "The saga of Dennis Kucinich: When one man stood up to

corporate power — in 1970s Cleveland" a synopsis by Chris Hedges of Kucinich's recently published book *The Division of Light and Power* for a good insight and background into Kucinich, who twice ran for the Democratic presidential nomination: https://www.salon.com/2021/07/23/the-saga-of-dennis-kucinich-when-one-man-stood-up-to-corporate-power--in-1970s-cleveland/

[106] See Emmett 2020, Holcombe 2020, Boettke et al. 2018, Burns 2016.

[107] See for example Owen 1939; Fisher 1920, 1936; Soddy 1933; Gesell 1958.

[108] Fisher (1936: xiii) wrote about the formation of a Currency Commission that 'would then have a standing like that of the Supreme Court, and become, as it were, a Supreme Court of Money'.

[109] www.monetary.org

[110] see: https://www.youtube.com/watch?v=0CaYuss28HQ

[111] see: https://www.congress.gov/bill/112th-congress/house-bill/2990

[112] This institution would resemble Fisher's Currency Commission discussed in Chapter 3

[113] Also see Dyson et al. 2016, 42, for a comprehensive description on how the conversion process could be managed.

[114] Sigurjonsson was a member of parliament for the Progressive Party from 2013 to 2016.

[115] A further report was commissioned by the Icelandic Prime minister's Office - see KPMG & Jourdan 2016 - which provides an overview (44 pages) of the issues raised by Sigurjonsson.

[116] See: KPMG & Jourdan, S 2016, for a summary of various sovereign enquiries into monetary reform.

[117] Letter from Keynes to Fisher, July 7, 1944, quoted in Allen 1993: 715 n49.

[118] See: https://www.gdi.ch/en

[119] See for example: Broadbent 2016, BOE 2020, BOE 2021 (b), BOE 2021 (c)

7 Conclusion pp. 164-172

[120] Keynes had. a different tack on this. He wrote in 1931: 'A considerable part of this "financing" takes place through the banking system, which interposes its guarantee between its depositors who lend it money, and its borrowing customers to whom it loans money wherewith to finance the purchase of real assets' (Keynes 1931; 59). Keynes contradicts Vanderlip (Columbia 1908) who does not talk about customers lending the bank money. He talks about the bank filling a customer 'need' for money simply by assessing their credit risk and once deemed worthwhile, creating the funds. Vanderlip was correct.

[121] As Seligman (Columbia 1908: xxvi) said about the wisdom and experience of the bankers that participated in that conference.

[122] Leacock was a Canadian political scientist who studied in Chicago under Veblen at the turn of the 19th century. He obtained his doctorate in political science and political economy.

Bibliography

Alcorn, A. 2014, 'The Political Climate in America from 1908 to 1913 the Birth of the Federal Reserve System', *The Virginia Tech Undergraduate Historical Review*, vol. 3.

Alford, R. 2010, *SOME HELP IN UNDERSTANDING BRITAIN'S BANKING CRISIS, 2007 – 09*, 193, Special Paper.

Akin, T. & Dolgun, M.H. 2016, 'The Chicago Plan from the Lenses of Islamic Finance: Implications for Financial Stability and Indebtedness', *International Journal of Islamic Economics and Finance Studies*, vol. 1, no. 2.

Allen, W.R. 1993, 'Irving Fisher and the 100 percent reserve proposal', *The Journal of Law and Economics*, vol. 36, no. 2, pp. 703–17.

Anderson, R.G., Bordo, M. & Duca, J.V. 2016, *Money and Velocity During Financial Crises: From the Great Depression to the Great Recession*, 22100, NBER Working Paper Series.

Angell, J.W. 1927, 'Wealth, Virtual Wealth and Debt. by Frederick Soddy - Review', *Political Science Quarterly*, vol. 42, no. 4, pp. 621–4.

Angell, J.W. 1935, 'The 100 Per Cent Reserve Plan', *The Quarterly Journal of Economics*, vol. 50, no. 1, pp. 1–35.

Askari, H. & Krichene, N. 2016, '100 Percent Reserve Banking and the Path to a Single-Country Gold Standard', *The Quarterly Journal of Austrian Economics*, no. 1, p. 37.

Auer, R & Boehme, R 2020, 'The technology of retail central bank digital currency', *BIS Quarterly Review*, p. 16.

Batchelder, R.W. & Glasner, D. 1991, *Pre-Keynesian Monetary Thories of the great Depression: Whatever happened to Hawtrey and Cassel?*, Working Paper No 626, Working Paper, University of California, Los Angeles.

Beneš, J. & Kumhof, M. 2012, *The Chicago plan revisited*, viewed 20 May 2017, <https://papers.ssrn.com/sol3/papers.cfm?abstract_id=2169748>.

Bernanke, B.S. 2010, 'Aiding the economy: What the Fed did and why', *Washington Post*, 4 November, p. 3.

Bezemer, DJ 2016, 'Towards an "accounting view" on money, banking and the macroeconomy: history, empirics, theory', *Cambridge Journal of Economics*, vol. 40, no. 5, pp. 1275–1295.

BOE 2021 (a), 'Bank of England statement on Central Bank Digital Currency | Bank of England', accessed November 21, 2021, from <https://www.bankofengland.co.uk/news/2021/april/bank-of-england-statement-on-central-bank-digital-currency>.

BOE 2021 (b), 'New forms of digital money | Bank of England', accessed November 19, 2021, from <https://www.bankofengland.co.uk/paper/2021/new-forms-of-digital-money>.

Boettke, P.J., Salter, A.W. & Smith, D.J. 2018, 'Money as meta-rule: Buchanan's constitutional economics as a foundation for monetary stability', *Public Choice*, vol. 176, no. 3–4, pp. 529–55.

Bordo, M.D. & Wheelock, D.C. 2010, *THE PROMISE AND PERFORMANCE OF THE FEDERAL RESERVE AS LENDER OF LAST RESORT 1914-1933*, NBER Working Paper Series, Working Paper 16763, Federal Reserve Bank of Atlanta, viewed 16 July 2019, <http://www.nber.org/papers/w16763>.

Bordo, M.D. & Rockoff, H. 2011, *The Influence of Irving Fisher on Milton Friedman's Monetary Economics*, Working Paper 17267, NBER Working Paper Series.

Boyes, R. 2009, *Meltdown Iceland: Lessons on the World Financial Crisis from a Small Bankrupt Island - REVIEW.*

Broadbent, B 2016, 'Central banks and digital currencies', *Speech at London School of Economics*, accessed July 31, 2017, from <http://www.

lse.ac.uk/website-archive/publicEvents/pdf/2016-LT/20160302-Dr-Ben-Broadbent-Transcript.pdf>.

Buchanan, J.M. 2010, 'THE CONSTITUTIONALIZATION OF MONEY', *Cato Journal*, vol. 30, no. 2, pp. 251–8.

Burgin, A. 2009, 'THE RADICAL CONSERVATISM OF FRANK H. KNIGHT', *Modern Intellectual History*, vol. 6, no. 03, p. 513.

Burns, S. 2016, 'Old (Chicago) school, new century: the link between Knight and Simons' Chicago plan to Buchanan's constitutional money', *Constitutional Political Economy*, vol. 27, no. 3, pp. 299–318.

Carpenter, S. & Demiralp, S. 2012, 'Money, reserves, and the transmission of monetary policy: Does the money multiplier exist?', *Journal of macroeconomics*, vol. 34, no. 1, pp. 59–75.

Chick, V. 1992, 'The Evolution of the Banking System and the Theory of Saving, Investment and Interest', in P. Arestis & S.C. Dow (eds),*On Money, Method and Keynes*, Palgrave Macmillan UK, London, pp. 193–205, viewed 29 May 2018, <http://link.springer.com/10.1007/978-1-349-21935-3_12>.

Chick, V. 2013, 'The Current Banking Crisis in the UK: An Evolutionary View.', *Financial Crises and the Nature of Capitalist Money*, Palgrave Macmillan UK, London U.K., pp. 148–61

Columbia 1908, *The Currency Problem and the Present Financial Situation*, Columbia University Press, New York, N.Y.

Cowan, D. 2016, *Frank H. Knight: prophet of freedom*, Great thinkers in economics, Palgrave Macmillan, Basingstoke.

Currie, L.B. (ed.) 1938, 'The 100 percent reserve plan':, *Journal of Economic Studies*, vol. 31, no. 3/4, pp. 355–65.

Daly, H.E. 1980, 'The economic thought of Frederick Soddy', *History of Political Economy*, vol. 12, no. 4, pp. 469–88.

Davenport, J. 1946, 'The Testament of Henry Simons', *The University of Chicago Law Review*, vol. 14, no. 1, pp. 5-14

Davies, G. 2002, *A history of money: from ancient times to the present day*, 3rd ed., with revisions., University of Wales Press, Cardiff.

Dawnay, E 2017, *Sovereign Money Initiative: The Background to the National Referendum on Sovereign Money in switzerland*, Verein Monetäre Modernisierung (MoMo), accessed from <www.Vollgeld-Initiative.ch/en>.

Demeulemeester, S 2018, 'The 100% money proposal and its implications for banking: the Currie–Fisher approach versus the Chicago Plan approach', *The European Journal of the History of Economic Thought*, vol. 25, no. 2, pp. 357–387.

Dimand, R.W. 2005, 'Fisher, Keynes, and the Corridor of Stability', *American Journal of Economics and Sociology*, vol. 64, no. 1, pp. 185–99.

Douglas, P.H., Fisher, I., Graham, F.D., Hamilton, E.J., King, W.I. & Whittlesey, C.R. 1939, *A PROGRAM FOR MONETARY REFORM*, p. 29.

Doukas, D. 2014, 'Epilogue: The Neoliberal Con', in E.P. Durrenberger & G. Palsson (eds),*Gambling Debt: Iceland's Rise and Fall in the Global Economy*, University Press of Colorado, pp. 217–25, viewed 10 November 2021, <http://upcolorado.com/university-press-of-colorado/item/2041-gambling-debt>.

Dow, S., Johnsen, G. & Montagnoli, A. 2015, *A critique of full reserve banking*, Sheffield Economic Research Paper Series, Research Paper, The University of Sheffield, Sheffield U.K

Dyson, B., Hodgson, G. & Lerven, F. van 2016, *Sovereign Money - An Introduction*, Positive Money, London, U.K.

Dyson, B & Hodgson, G 2016, 'Digital Cash: Why Central Banks Should Start Issuing Electronic Money', *Positive Money*, p. 44.

Emmett, R.B. 2009, *Frank Knight and the Chicago School in American Economics*, Routledge, Taylor & Francis Group, London ; New York.

Emmett, R.B. 2020, 'James M. Buchanan and Frank H. Knight on democracy as "government by discussion"', *Public Choice*, vol. 183, no. 3–4, pp. 303–14.

FCIC, 2010, *The Financial Crisis: Inquiry Report* 2010 .

FED BG 1939, *The Federal Reserve System: Its Purposes and Functions 1939*, Board of Governors of the Federal Reserve System (U.S.), Washington D.C.

FED BG 1943, *Banking and Monetary Statistics 1914-1941 Part I*, Board of Governors, Washington, D.C, viewed 2 December 2019, <https://fraser.stlouisfed.org/title/banking-monetary-statistics-1914-1941-38/part-i-6408>.

FED BG 1976, *Banking and Monetary Statistics 1941-1970*, Board of Governors, Washington, D.C, viewed 2 December 2019, <https://fraser.stlouisfed.org/files/docs/publications/bms/1941-1970/BMS41-70_complete.pdf>.

FED BG 2022, 'Money and Payments: The U.S. Dollar in the Age of Digital Transformation', , p. 40. Accessed from https://www.federalreserve.gov/publications/money-and-payments-discussion-paper.htm

FED Chicago 1994, *Modern Money Mechanics: A Workbook on Bank Reserves and Deposit Expansion*, Federal Reserve Bank of Chicago, Chicago, Ill.

Federici, S. 2014, 'From Commoning to Debt: Financialization, Micro-Credit and the Changing Architecture of Capital Accumulation', *South Atlantic Quarterly*, p. 17.

Felkerson, J. 2011, '$29,000,000,000,000: A Detailed Look at the Fed's Bailout by Funding Facility and Recipient', *SSRN Electronic Journal*, viewed 5 April 2018, <http://www.ssrn.com/abstract=1970414>.

Fishback, P. 2010, 'US monetary and fiscal policy in the 1930s', *Oxford Review of Economic Policy*, vol. 26, no. 3, pp. 385–413.

Fisher, I. 1907, *The Rate of Interest*, The Macmillan Company, New York, N.Y.

Fisher, I. 1912, *How to Invest When Prices Are Rising*, G. Lynn Sumner & Company, Scranton, Pa.

Fisher, I. 1920, *Stabilizing the Dollar*, The Macmillan Company, New York, N.Y.

Fisher, I. 1922 (1911), *The Purchasing Power of Money, its Determination and Relation to Credit, Interest and Crises*, Macmillan & Co, New York, N.Y.

Fisher, I., Mitchell, W.C., Palyi, M., Mitchell, W.F., Knight, F.H. & Karsten, K.G. 1927, 'Interest Theory and Price Movements--Discussion',

The American Economic Review, vol. 17, no. 1, pp. 106–22.

Fisher, I. 1933, 'The Debt-Deflation Theory of Great Depressions', *Econometrica*, vol. 1, no. 4, pp. 337–57.

Fisher, I. 1936, *100% Money*, Revised., Adelphi Company, New Rochelle, N.Y.

Fontana, G. & Sawyer, M. 2016, 'Full Reserve Banking: More "Cranks" Than "Brave Heretics"', *Cambridge Journal of Economics*, vol. 40, no. 5, pp. 1333–50.

Formaini, R.L. 2002, 'FRANK H. KNIGHT Origins of the Chicago School of Economics', *Economic Insights*, vol. 7, no. 3, p. 4.

Friedman, M. (1960), *A Program for Monetary Stability*, Fordham University Press, New York, N.Y.

Friedman, M. 1967, 'The Monetary Theory and Policy of Henry Simons', *The Journal of Law and Economics*, vol. 10, pp. 1–13.

Fuller, EW 2018, 'KEYNES_AND_FRACTIONAL_RESERVE_.pdf', *Procesos de Mercado: Revista Europea de Economía Política*, vol. 15, no. 1, pp. 39–74.

Galbraith, J.K. 2009, *The great crash*, 1929, Houghton Mifflin Harcourt, Boston, M.A.

Gesell, S. 1958, *The NATURAL ECONOMIC ORDER*, trans. P. Pye, Peter Owen Limited, London U.K.

Goodhart, C.A.E. 1989, *Money, information, and uncertainty*, 2nd ed., Macmillan, Houndmills, Basingstoke, Hampshire.

Goodhart, C.A. & Jensen, M.A. 2015, 'A Commentary on Patrizio Lainà's "Proposals for Full-Reserve Banking: A Historical Survey from David Ricardo to Martin Wolf"', *Economic Thought*, vol. 4, no. 2, pp. 20–31.

Goodhart, C.A.E. 2017, 'The Determination of the Money Supply: Flexibility Versus Control: Determination of the Money Supply', *The Manchester School*, vol. 85, pp. 33–56.

Graham, FD 1936, 'Partial Reserve Money and the 100 Per Cent Proposal', *The American Economic Review*, vol. 26, no. 3, pp. 428–440.

Griffin, GE 1998, *The creature from Jekyll Island: a second look at the* *federal reserve* 3rd ed., American Media, Westlake Village, CA.

Groseclose, E.E. 1976 [1934], *Money and man: a survey of monetary experience*, 4th ed., rev.enl. by the author., University of Oklahoma Press, Norman.

Hart, A.G. 1935, 'A Proposal for Making Monetary Management Effective in the United States', *The Review of Economic Studies*, vol. 2, no. 2, pp. 104-115.

Hart, A.G. & Mehrling, P. 1995, Debt, crisis, and recovery: the 1930s and the 1990s, Columbia University seminar series, M. E. Sharpe, Armonk, NY.

Hicks, J.R. 1935, 'A Suggestion for Simplifying the Theory of Money', *Economica*, vol. 2, no. 5, p. 1.

Holcombe, R.G. 2020, 'James M. Buchanan's constitutional project: past and future', *Public Choice*, vol. 183, no. 3–4, pp. 371–87.

Hollis, C. 1937, *The Breakdown of Money: An Historical Explanation*, Sheed and Ward, London U.K.

H.R.2990 - 112th Congress (2011-2012): National Emergency Employment Defense Act of 2011." *Congress.gov*, Library of Congress, 8 May 2012, https://www.congress.gov/bill/112th-congress/house-bill/2990/committees.

Huber, J. 2015, *The Chicago Plan (100% Reserve) and Plain Sovereign Money*, viewed 13 June 2017, <sovereignmoney.eu/the-chicago-plan-100-per- cent-reserve-and-plain-sovereign- money>.

Huber, J. 2017 (a), *Sovereign Money: Beyond Reserve Banking*, Palgrave Macmillan, Cham, Ch, viewed 5 March 2018, <http://link.springer.com/10.1007/978-3-319-42174-2>.

Huber, J. 2017 (b), 'Split-circuit reserve banking–functioning, dysfunctions and future perspectives', *real-world economics review*, no. 80, p. 63.

Huber, J. 2017 (c), *What is Sovereign Money*, p. 8.

Huber, J 2019, 'Digital currency. Design principles to support a shift from bankmoney to central bank digital currency', *real-world economics review*, no. 88, pp. 76–90.

Icelandic Parliament 2016, *Icelandic Parliamentary resolution on reforming the mechanism of monetary creation.*, accessed from <http://positivemoney.org/wp-content/uploads/2016/02/Parliamentary_resolution_EN.pdf>.

Ingham, G 2004, 'The nature of money', *Economic Sociology: European Electronic Newsletter*, vol. 5, no. 2, pp. 18–28.

Ingham, G.K. 2008, *Capitalism*, Polity, Cambridge ; Malden, MA.

Jackson, A 2013, *Sovereign Money: paving the way for a sustainable recovery*, Positive Money, London, U.K.

Jakab, Z. & Kumhof, M. 2019, 'Banks are Not Intermediaries of Loanable Funds — Facts, Theory and Evidence', *SSRN Electronic Journal*, viewed 1 July 2019, <https://www.ssrn.com/abstract=3274706>.

Juego, B. & Schmidt, J.D. 2009, 'Unpacking the Global Crisis: Neo-liberalism, Financial Crises, and Authoritarian Liberalism', *Sixth Historical Materialism Annual Conference 2009-" Another World is Necesary: Crisis, Struggle and Political Alternatives"*, viewed 20 September 2016, <http://vbn.aau.dk/ws/files/19017252/Juego-Schmidt_HM_2009_Paper.pdf>.

Johnson, R.T. 2010, *Historical Beginnings: The Federal Reserve*, Federal Reserve Bank of Boston, Boston, MA.

Johnson, S. & Kwak, J. 2010, *13 bankers: the Wall Street takeover and the next financial meltdown*, 1st ed., Pantheon Books, New York.

Jordà, Ò, Schularick, M & Taylor, AM 2014, *The great mortgaging: housing finance, crises and business cycles*, CESifo, Munich, Germany, accessed May 31, 2017, from <http://economicpolicy.oxfordjournals.org/content/31/85/107.abstract>.

Keynes, J.M. 1920, *The Economic Consequences of Peace*, Harcourt, Brace and Howe, New York.

Keynes, J.M. 1930, *A Treatise on Money vol I,* vol. 1, Macmillan & Co Limited, London U.K.

Keynes, J.M. 1931, *Essays in Persuasion*, Macmillan & Co Limited, London U.K.

Keynes, J.M. 1936, *General theory of employment, interest and money*, Macmillan & Co Limited, London, U.K.

Kindleberger, C.P. & Aliber, R.Z. 2005, *Manias, panics, and crashes: a history of financial crises*, Wiley investment classics, 5th ed., John Wiley & Sons, Hoboken, N.J

Knight, F.H. 1921, *Risk, uncertainty and profit*, Houghton Mifflin Company, Boston, MA.

Knight, F.H. 1927, 'Review of Frederick Soddy's Wealth, Virtual Wealth, and Debt.', *The Saturday Review of Literature*, April 16 1927, p. 732.

Knight, F.H., Simons, H.C., Cox, G.V., Douglas, P.H., Director, A., Mints, L.W., Hart, A.G. & Schulz, H. 1933, *The Chicago Plan for Banking Reform*, March 1933.

Knight, F.H. 1937, 'Unemployment: And Mr. Keynes's Revolution in Economic Theory', *The Canadian Journal of Economics and Political Science*, vol. 3, no. 1, p. 100.

Knight, F.H. 1960, *Intelligence and Democratic Action*, Harvard University Press, Cambridge Massachusetts.

Kohn, D.L. 2010, T*he Federal Reserve's Policy Actions during the Financial Crisis and Lessons for the Future*, Speech, Board of Governors of the Federal Reserve System, Carleton University Ottawa, Canada.

KPMG & Jourdan, S. 2016, *Money Issuance: Alternative Monetary Systems*, Reykjavik, Iceland

Lainà, P. 2015, 'Proposals for full-reserve banking: A historical survey from David Ricardo to Martin Wolf', *Economic Thought*, vol. 4, no. 2, pp. 1–19.

Laeven, L. & Valencia, F. 2012, *Systemic banking crises database: An update.*

Lawson, T. 1988, 'Probability and Uncertainty in Economic Analysis', *Journal of Post Keynesian Economics*, vol. 11, no. 1, pp. 38–65.

Lþingis, RAA 2010, 'Causes of the Collapse of the Icelandic Banks - Responsibility, Mistakes and Negligence' available from: https://www.rna.is/media/skjol/RNAvefurKafli21Enska.pdf

Leeson, R. (ed.) 2003, *Keynes, Chicago, and Friedman Volume 1*, Pickering & Chatto, London.

Leeson, R. (ed.) 2003, *Keynes, Chicago, and Freedman Volume 2*, Pickering & Chatto, London.

Lindbergh, C.A. 1913, *Banking and currency and the money trust*, National Capital Press Inc., Washington D.C.

Marx, K. 1909, *Capital: A Critique of Political Economy. Volume III: The Process of Capitalist Production as a Whole [1894]*, F. Engels (ed.), trans. E. Untermann, Charles H. Kerr & Company, Chicago, Ill.

McLeay, M., Radia, A. & Thomas, R. 2014, 'Money creation in the modern economy', *Bank of England*, viewed 4 May 2017, <https://papers.ssrn.com/sol3/papers.cfm?abstract_id=2416234>.

Mehrling, P. 2011, *The new Lombard Street: how the Fed became the dealer of last resort*, Princeton University Press, Princeton, N.J.

Mehrling, P., Pozsar, Z., Sweeney, J. & Neilson, D.H. 2013, 'Bagehot was a Shadow Banker: Shadow Banking, Central Banking, and the Future of Global Finance', *SSRN Electronic Journal*, viewed 4 April 2019, <http://www.ssrn.com/abstract=2232016>.

Merricks, L. 1996, *The world made new: Frederick Soddy, science, politics, and environment (Fischer)*, Oxford University Press, Oxford ; New York.

Minsky, H.P. 1957, 'Central Banking and Money Market Changes', *Hyman P. Minsky Archive. Paper 194.*, p. 10.

Minsky, H.P. 1964, 'Longer waves in financial relations: financial factors in the more severe depressions', *The American Economic Review*, vol. 54, no. 3, pp. 324–35.

Minsky, H.P. 1970, *Towards a Meaningful Macro Model of the Economy*, Paper 368, Archive Paper, Bard Digital Commons.

Minsky, H.P. 1986, *Stabilising an Unstable Economy*, Yale University Press.

Minsky, H.P. 1992, The financial instability hypothesis, viewed 15 August 2017, <https://papers.ssrn.com/sol3/papers.cfm?abstract_id=161024>.

Minsky, H.P. 1998, 'Financial Instability and the Decline (?) of Banking: Public Policy Implications', *SSRN Electronic Journal*, viewed 21 June 2018, <http://www.ssrn.com/abstract=100888>.

Mises, L. von 1912, *The Theory of Money and Credit*, Yale University Press, New Haven, viewed 1 April 2017, <https://mises.org/sites/default/files/The%20Theory%20of%20Money%20and%20Credit_3.pdf>.

Moore, H.L. 1909, 'The Currency Problem and the Present Financial Situation - REVIEW', *The Economic Journal*, vol. 19, no. 74, pp. 253–5. http://www.jstor.com/stable/2221443

National Emergency Employment Defense Act of 2011 2011 **(H.R. 2990)**. Accessed from https://www.congress.gov/bill/112th-congress/house-bill/2990

Nikitin, P.I. 1983, *The Fundamentals of Political Economy*, trans. J. Sayer, Progress Publishers, Moscow, Ru.

Owen, R.L. 1939, *AN EXPOSITION OF THE PRINCIPLES-OF MODERN MONETARY SCIENCE IN THEIR REVATION TO THE NATIONAL ECONOMY AND THE BANKING SYSTEM OF THE UNITED STATES*, National Economy and the Banking System of the United States, 28, Congressional Report, 76th Congress 1st Session.

Papadimitriou, D.B. (ed.) 1996, *Stability in the Financial System*, Palgrave Macmillan UK, London, viewed 11 June 2021, <http://link.springer.com/10.1007/978-1-349-24767-7>.

Phillips, A.S. 2014, 'BANK-CREATED MONEY, MONETARY SOVEREIGNTY, AND THE FEDERAL DEFICIT: TOWARD A NEW PARADIGM IN THE GOVERNMENT-SPENDING DEBATE', *WESTERN NEW ENGLAND LAW REVIEW*, vol. 36, no. 3, pp. 221–60.

Phillips, R.J. 1992, *The Chicago Plan'and New Deal Banking Reform*, viewed 20 May 2017, <https://papers.ssrn.com/sol3/papers.cfm?abstract_id=160989>.

Phillips, R.J. 1995, *The Chicago plan & New Deal banking reform*, M.E. Sharpe, Armonk, N.Y.

Polanyi, K. 1957 [1944], *The great transformation*, Beacon Pres, Boston, MA., viewed 21 September 2016, <http://library.mpib-berlin.mpg.de/toc/z2010_3.pdf>.

***Popular initiative 'For crisis-safe money**: Money creation by the National Bank only! (Sovereign Money Initiative)'* n.d., viewed 29 May 2018,

<https://www.admin.ch/gov/en/start/documentation/votes/20180610/Sovereign-Money-Initiative.html>.

Quigley, C. 1966, *Tragedy and Hope: A History of the World in our Time*, Macmillan, New York, N.Y.

Ravn, I. 2021, 'How financial bubbles are fueled by money creation a.k.a. bank lending: An explanation for public education', *Real-World Economics Review*, no. 97, pp. 143–54.

Richards, T 2020, 'Retail Central Bank Digital Currency: Design Considerations and Rationales | Speeches', *Reserve Bank of Australia*, accessed October 14, 2020, from <https://www.rba.gov.au/speeches/2020/sp-so-2020-10-14.html>.

Schumpeter, J.A. 1939, *BUSINESS CYCLES: A Theoretical, Historical and Statistical Analysis of the Capitalist Process*, McGraw-Hill Book Company, New York, N.Y, viewed 14 January 2017, <http://classiques.uqac.ca/classiques/Schumpeter_joseph/business_cycles/schumpeter_business_cycles.pdf>.

Schumpeter, J.A. 1954, *History of economic analysis*, Allen & Unwin Publishers, London, viewed 1 February 2017, <http://public.eblib.com/choice/publicfullrecord.aspx?p=256868>.

Sheard, P. 2013, 'Repeat After Me: Banks Cannot And Do Not" Lend Out" Reserves', *Standard & Poors Ratings Direct*.

Shiller, R.J. 2013, 'IRVING FISHER, DEBT DEFLATION, AND CRISES', *Journal of the History of Economic Thought*, vol. 35, no. 02, pp. 179–83.

Sigurjonsson, F 2015, 'Monetary Reform: A better monetary system for Iceland', accessed from <https://www.stjornarradid.is/media/forsaetisraduneyti-media/media/Skyrslur/monetary-reform.pdf>.

Simons, H.C. 1936, 'Rules versus Authorities in Monetary Policy', *Journal of Political Economy*, vol. 44, no. 1, pp. 1–30.

Simons, H.C. 1948, *Economic Policy for a Free Society*, The University of Chicago Press, Chicago, Ill.

Singleton, J. 2010, *Central Banking in the Twentieth Century*, Cambridge University Press, Cambridge, viewed 4 December 2016, <http://ebooks.cambridge.org/ref/id/CBO9780511782053>.

SMIC 2018, *Clarifications_to_SNBs_FAQ_on_Sovereign_Money.pdf*, viewed 15 March 2021, <https://www.vollgeld-initiative.ch/fa/img/English/Clarifications_to_SNBs_FAQ_on_Sovereign_Money.pdf>.

Smithin, J. 2013, 'Credit creation, the monetary circuit and the formal validity of money', *Monetary Economies of Production*, Edward Elgar Publishing, pp. 41–53, viewed 22 July 2021, <http://www.elgaronline.com/view/9781781003947.00015.xml>.

Smithin, J. 2016, 'Some puzzles about money, finance and the monetary circuit', *Cambridge Journal of Economics*, vol. 40, no. 5, pp. 1259–74.

Soddy, F. 1922, *Cartesian economics: the bearing of physical science upon state stewardship*, Hendersons.

Soddy, F. 1933, *Wealth, Virtual Wealth and Debt: The Solution of the Economic Paradox*, 3rd edn, Britons Publishing Company, London England.

St Germain, F. 1984, Inquiry into Continental Illinois Corp. and Continental Illinois National Bank 1984 (U.S. Government Printing Office).

Stock Exchange Practices 1934 (U.S. Government Printing Office). Retrieved from https://archive.org/details/stockexchangepra1433unit

Tavlas, G.S. 2020, *On the Controversy Over the Origins of the Chicago Plan for 100 Percent Reserves: Sorry, Frederick Soddy, it was Knight and (Most Probably) Simons!**, Economics Working Paper 20102, Working Paper, Hoover Institution, Stanford, CA.

Taylor, A.M. 2012, *The great leveraging*, 398, BIS Working Paper.

Tobin, J. (1985), 'Financial Innovation and Deregulation in Perspective', Bank of Japan Monetary and Economic Studies, III, pp. 19-29, as re printed in J. Tobin, Policies for Prosperity, Cambridge, MA: MIT Press, 1987, pp. 255-64

Tobin, J 1987, 'A Case for Preserving Regulatory Distinctions', *Challenge*, vol. 30, no. 5, pp. 10–17.

Tobin, J. 2005, 'Irving Fisher (1867–1947)', *American Journal of Economics and Sociology*, vol. 64, no. 1, pp. 19–42.

Turner, A. 2010, 'What do banks do? Why do credit booms and busts occur and what can public policy do about it', *The future of finance*, vol. 5.

Turner, A. 2016, *Between debt and the devil: money, credit, and fixing global finance*, Princeton University Press, Princeton.

Valencia, F., FValencia@imf.org, Laeven, L., & LLaeven@imf.org 2008, 'Systemic Banking Crises: A New Database', *IMF Working Papers*, vol. 08, no. 224, p. 1.

Vanderlip, F.A. 1913, *A Plan for a Government Central Bank*, Speech, Investment Bankers association of America, Chicago, Ill.

Van Dixhoorn, C. 2013, 'Full Reserve Banking', *Sustainable Finance Lab.[Retrieved from]*, viewed 20 May 2017, <http://www.sustainablefinancelab.nl/files/2013/07/Full-Reserve-Banking-Dixhoorn-SFL.pdf>.

Van Horn, R. & Emmett, R.B. 2015, 'Two trajectories of democratic capitalism in the post-war Chicago school: Frank Knight versus Aaron Director', *Cambridge Journal of Economics*, vol. 39, no. 5, pp. 1443–55.

Vercelli, A. 2017, *Crisis and Sustainability*, Palgrave Macmillan UK, London, viewed 12 August 2021, <http://link.springer.com/10.1057/978-1-137-60069-1>.

Vercelli, A. 2019, *Finance and Democracy: Towards a Sustainable Financial System*, Springer International Publishing, Cham, viewed 11 June 2021, <http://link.springer.com/10.1007/978-3-030-27912-7>.

VOLLGELD-INITIATIVE SCHWEIZ: *English* - 2018, viewed 2 September 2021, <https://www.vollgeld-initiative.ch/english/>.

Wade, R.H. & Sigurgeirsdottir, S. 2012, 'Iceland's rise, fall, stabilisation and beyond', *Cambridge Journal of Economics*, vol. 36, no. 1, pp. 127–44.

Warburg, P. 1913, 'The Owen-Glass Bill as submitted to the Democratic Caucus', *North American Review Publishing Co*, p. 20.

Werner, R.A. 2014, 'How do banks create money, and why can other firms not do the same? An explanation for the coexistence of lending and deposit-taking', *International Review of Financial Analysis*, vol. 36, pp. 71–7.

Werner, R.A. 2016, 'A lost century in economics: Three theories of banking and the conclusive evidence', *International Review of Financial*

Analysis, vol. 46, pp. 361–79.

Whalen, C.J. 1988, 'The Minsky-Simons Connection: A Neglected Thread in the History of Economic Thought', *Journal of Economic Issues*, vol. 22, no. 2, pp. 533–44.

Wicksell, K. 1936, *Interest and prices: a study of the causes regulating the value of money*, Sentry Press, New York, N.Y.

Wicksell, K. 1978, *Letures on Political Economy Vol 2: Money*, Lectures on political economy, Reprinted., Routledge, London.

Withers, H. 1920, *The Meaning of Money*, EP Dutton & Company, New York, N.Y.

Wray, L.R. 1993, 'Introduction to an Alternative History of Money', *SSRN - Levy Economics Institute, Working Papers Series*The origins of money and the development of the modern financial system, viewed 15 October 2016, <http://papers.ssrn.com/sol3/papers.cfm?abstract_id=150948>.

Wray L. Randall 2014, 'DEBT-FREE MONEY: A NON-SEQUITUR IN SEARCH OF A POLICY | New Economic Perspectives', accessed January 19, 2022, from <https://neweconomicperspectives.org/2014/07/debt-free-money-non-sequitur-search-policy.html>.

Wray, L.R. 2015, *DEBT-FREE MONEY AND BANANA REPUBLICS | New Economic Perspectives*, viewed 20 January 2022, <https://neweconomicperspectives.org/2015/12/debt-free-money-banana-republics.html>.

Yamaguchi, K 2011, 'Workings of A Public Money System of Open Macroeconomies', in *Modeling the American Monetary Act Completed. Paper at the 29th International Conference of the System Dynamics Society, Washington DC*, accessed August 9, 2017, from <http://monetary.org/wp-content/uploads/2011/11/DesignOpenMacro.pdf>.

Yamaguchi, K. 2019, *Money and Macroeconomic Dynamics: Accounting System Dynamics Approach*, 4th edn, Japan Futures Research Center, Awaji Island, Japan.

Yeager, L.B. (ed.) 1962, *In Search of a Monetary Constitution*, Harvard University Press, Cambridge, MA

Zarlenga, S.A. 2002, *The Lost Science of Money: The Mythology of*

Money - The Story of Power, American Monetary Institute, Valatie, N.Y., viewed 24 May 2017, <https://murdercube.com/files/Money/Lost%20Science%20of%20Money/Lost%20Science%20of%20Money.pdf>.

Zarlenga, S.A. 2010, Presenting the American Monetary Act (as of July 18, 2010), American Monetary Institute.

Figures and Tables

Tables

Index

Page numbers in bold refer to figures and tables: f denotes figures, t denotes tables. Titles of books and acts are given in italics.

www.ingramcontent.com/pod-product-compliance
Lightning Source LLC
LaVergne TN
LVHW050911210926
848482LV00012B/406
* 9 7 8 1 9 2 3 6 0 1 0 7 9 *